MW01504539

Listening to Light

Listening to Light

Love Letters from Walking with Spirit

Award Winning Author
Dr. Ruth Anderson

Listening to Light: Love Letters from Walking with Spirit
Published by SageHouse Press
Louisville, CO

Copyright ©2019 Ruth Anderson. All rights reserved.

No part of this book may be reproduced in any form or by any mechanical means, including information storage and retrieval systems without permission in writing from the publisher/author, except by a reviewer who may quote passages in a review.

All images, logos, quotes, and trademarks included in this book are subject to use according to trademark and copyright laws of the United States of America.

Publisher's Cataloging-in-Publication data

Names: Anderson, Ruth Elaine (1960-), author.
Title: Listening to light : love letters from walking with spirit / by Dr. Ruth Anderson.
Description: First trade paperback original edition. | Louisville [Colorado] : SageHouse Press, 2019. Also being published as an ebook.
Identifiers: ISBN 978-0-9984573-4-5
Subjects: LCSH: Spiritualism. | Archangels. | Spirituality--New Age movement.
BISAC: BODY, MIND & SPIRIT / Healing / Prayer & Spiritual. BODY, MIND & SPIRIT / Angels & Spirit Guides.
Classification: LCC BF1275.F3 | DDC 133–dc22

Cover Artwork by Valerieann Giovanni

QUANTITY PURCHASES: Schools, companies, professional groups, clubs, and other organizations may qualify for special terms when ordering quantities of this title. For information, email SageHousePress@gmail.com

Book is printed in the United States of America.

All rights reserved by Ruth Anderson and SageHouse Press.

This book is lovingly dedicated to my beautiful friends and family.

To my colleagues, thank you each for following your calling
and for walking with me in mine.

Divine Mother, I have never felt such unconditional love.
May your grace be felt through these pages.

Table of Contents

Foreword

Doctor Ruth Anderson is a gifted spiritual guide and healer with remarkable intuitive gifts. After meeting her through a mutual friend, Ruth interviewed me twice for her Divine Mother podcast series. Throughout the interview process, we became acquainted and quickly discovered a deep spiritual resonance.

In her third and most recent book, *Listening to Light: Love Letters from Walking with Spirit*, she illuminates the important process of going within, and listening to Spirit. She provides readers with a beautiful and simple model for receiving guidance and information on all things, large and small.

Sometimes, in the pressures and busyness of modern life, it can seem as though there is no time for connection with Spirit. Yet, through reading the text of Ruth's inner dialogues with the Divine Mother and her angelic guides, the reader can easily see how to weave a regular spiritual connection into everyday life. Ruth also shares her easy to follow methods for clarifying the information and guidance she receives. Her methods are exceptionally practical and can be used for shifting emotional states as well as for getting profound guidance.

Throughout the book, Ruth takes you on a journey of living life from a place of divine guidance, and makes it seem eminently doable and desirable. It is my great honor and pleasure to introduce this truly inspiring, heart-opening book.

In closing, I asked the Divine Mother if she wanted to add something to this foreword. She shared that "I send my love and blessings to all the readers, and shine my light into their hearts for greater guidance as they walk on their spiritual journey."

~**Sumaya O'Grady, MS**
Oracle Priestess, Soul Alchemist
Co-author of *Come out of Hiding and Shine* and *Becoming Outrageously Successful.*
www.Amazon.com/author/sumayaogrady
Sumaya@SouldeepConfidence.com

From the Author

I was interviewed by Sarah Jeane on *Love the Angels*, HealthyLife. net Radio on 9.27.17. I received a message that day that I'd like to share with all of you.

Sarah Jeane: "Do you have any last messages that you would like to share with the listeners?"

Ruth: "So I'm just listening to my guides right now, and the message that I'm getting is from Divine Mother. The message from Divine Mother is that there is so much love that is available to people if they will just connect in [with the Spiritual Divinity]. That it's as easy as just sitting quietly and opening your mind and your heart and asking the Divine Mother, or any of the archangels, to please be with you. It's that easy.

"Archangel Raphael and Archangel Michael are asking that people put on armor; that people put on their armor and go stand out in the world and share their truth. It's people's truth that is going to make an impact in our world today. So, don't be afraid to gird yourself with the armor of the angels and your own truth. Go put yourself out in the world even when it's not comfortable. Go share your truth."

This book is a call to action. If you read those last two paragraphs and thought, "I got it. I know and love the Spiritual Divinity, and I am already speaking my truth about Spirit and my place in the world as a lightworker," then don't read any further. Put the book down, or better yet, hand it to someone else who could benefit from it and get back to your calling of helping guide others to higher levels of vibrational frequency and divine light. The world needs you standing in your strength providing your gifts and talents right now. Know you are not alone, and that together our love and commitment is huge! Much love to you on your journey!

If the message from the Spiritual Divinity is foreign or mystifying, then please continue reading. And welcome home.

chapter one

Love Letters

Don't do, just be. Don't think, just listen. Don't seek, just love.
-Divine Mother

Welcome. As you enter the stories in this book, please allow yourself to get caught up in the wonder, the questions, and the possibilities. Feel free to exhale. Take breaks to meditate or pray if something on these pages sends you inward or upward.

If you read something that makes you question what you thought you knew, embrace that. Remember, you don't need to believe everything you think.

Each of these learning opportunities felt like Spirit had written me a love letter or given me an immense gift. Sometimes I laughed, sometimes I was stunned, and sometimes it brought tears to my eyes. I not only felt a connection to an energy that was different and bigger than mine, but I also gained an incredible understanding of life, death, and my very existence as both a spiritual being and a spiritual being *in* a physical body. With each lesson, I felt love, acceptance, and belonging in this experience that we call life.

Each lesson felt like a message from a trusted loved one. Although there were a few times I was caught off guard, I was never stretched beyond my ability to comprehend, and never feared for my safety. Frankly, the only fear I had was of my own inadequacy to comprehend and interpret the messages well, so they could reach people who would benefit from them.

I always knew that what I was learning was for the greater good, that these messages were to be shared so that others could learn and grow as a result. Archangel Michael told me that not everyone would welcome or understand my messages. I ultimately agreed and appreciated the heads up. I am not here to proselytize or persuade anyone of anything. I am merely sharing that which I have observed and been told through communication with Spirit.

What about the times that I received a message of tough love? Why would I include those comments in this book? Of course, I would prefer to make myself look perfect, after all, who could possibly know the difference? But, that would not be an accurate portrayal of my relationship with Divine Mother or the archangels. I have chosen to stand in integrity and provide authentic conversations as they happened, warts and all.

These lessons, these love letters, were shared in love with me; and with heartfelt connection, I now give them to you. I pray that this book makes you feel like you, personally, have spent time with Divine Mother, the archangels, and God. If my messages and connection to the Spiritual Divinity resonate with you, I welcome you to join me on this journey.

The Big Picture

My family and I vacationed on Sanibel Island several years ago. I am an avid beachcomber and would walk up and down the beach with my head down looking at shell after shell. I stooped to pick them up, feel their smooth or jagged edges, examine the colors, and put them back on the ground. I spent four days doing nothing more than watching my daughters play on the beach, walking, and staring at the shells on the ground. I loved it! Even when our young girls napped, I would stare out at the ocean from our second story condo. I didn't want to lose a minute of our time at the ocean.

One morning, I woke early and went to the big picture windows to watch the sunrise. I noticed some people walking on the beach. Each of them was doing just what I had done on the beach. Walking, head down, focused solely on the shells underfoot. But from my second story vantage point, my eyes were drawn past the shell hunters. A pod of 12 or so dolphins was swimming and jumping quite close to shore. The folks hunting for shells completely missed the beautiful display of the dolphins. What a good life lesson that was for me!

This story about the shells and dolphins makes me think about how my spiritual journey is different than many people's journeys. Most folks seem wrapped up in the myopic details of daily life, or are stooped over looking for shells, not taking a break to look at things on the horizon and out of reach. During the past five years, I have grown spiritually, learning to understand and walk with Spirit. This has been possible because I have the luxury of being retired and am able to be open to all that Spirit allows me to learn, without the responsibilities or time commitments of a job. I have not only been able to observe the dolphins in the background, or in my case, the Spiritual Divinity, but have been able to know them, talk with them, and listen to them. Not everyone understands my fascination with seeing the big picture, but I wouldn't have it any other way.

Twins

As I worked on my second book, *Walking with Spirit*, I consciously sought guidance from Divine Mother and Archangel Gabriel. I was informed that I would be writing not one book, but two, at essentially the same time. While seeking clarification, Spirit showed me the concept of twins. I was to incubate two different books. I reminded Spirit that many authors take time to rest and refresh before beginning the next book. Sometimes there might be years in between books. It felt like a daunting task to write two books at the same time. I looked for stalling tactics.

I said, *"But even with twins, one is born before the other."*

"Yes, but they are both developing at the same time."

"Right." I contemplated the time commitment for my family and me. I finally agreed to give it a try. *"I am guessing if you are telling me this, there is a reason for it, and you can help me make it happen."*

The first book would be called *Walking with Spirit* and the second one would be called *Love Letters from Walking with Spirit*. (The second title would change, as I will detail later on.) I was shown that Walking with Spirit was being orchestrated by Archangel Michael and Love Letters from Walking with Spirit was being orchestrated by Divine Mother.

One day, as I was working on the books, I found it impossible to concentrate. My energy and attention were spun or pushed away from the book, as if by an unseen force. I was immediately exhausted and felt I had no other choice but to close my eyes. I half meditated and half dozed. I asked Archangel Metatron to help me manage my time because the timeframe for getting these two books published and into the world was short. In meditation, I was in a black universe; I saw and heard nothing. Then I was shown two shiny discs spinning against the black background.

I knew that each disc represented one of my books. I saw that while the disks were spinning I could not write without being spun out by their energetic force. I knew it was time for me to take a break from writing while the archangels prepared the books in the ethereal realm first. I needed to prepare myself to be in alignment with them.

A month later, I checked on the energy of the two spinning disks. The first one had changed; it was spinning more slowly and changing direction. It was filling itself with the energy of all my teachers who are mentioned in the book. I was shown the core energy within the book, which included the intense healing energy of God and Archangel Michael. Then the disk was surrounded by 1,000 souls. The spinning disk shattered and was carried off by the souls, piece by piece. Then there was only one spinning disk left, representing this book.

YIN AND YANG

 As *Walking with Spirit* was nearing completion, I had a reading with my lightworker friend Delphine. She read the energy of the twin books. She saw the energy of *Walking with Spirit* as deep blue and connected to Archangel Michael. I concurred. She read the second twin as holding Divine Mother's energy and swirling ethereal colors of milky purples and pinks. This matched with what I had been shown previously. She saw a whale's tail and wondered what the connection was to the second book. I shared that we would be heading to Nantucket in a few weeks and was hoping to get a great deal of writing accomplished there. As the small island used to be a hub of the whaling industry, the whale's tail is found on most Nantucket souvenirs. She also saw the Yin and Yang symbol representing the interconnection between the books. Each was capable of standing on its own but inextricably linked to the other.

I had forgotten about Delphine seeing the Yin and Yang symbol until I woke up with it on my mind. I looked on the internet for its meaning.

"The principle of Yin and Yang is that all things exist as inseparable and contradictory opposites, for example, female-male, dark-light and old-young. The principle, dating from the 3rd century BCE or even earlier, is a fundamental concept in Chinese philosophy and culture in general. The two opposites of Yin and Yang attract and complement each other and, as their symbol illustrates, each side has at its core an element of the other (represented by the small dots). Neither pole is superior to the other and, as an increase in one brings a corresponding decrease in the other, a correct balance between the two poles must be reached in order to achieve harmony." https://www.ancient.eu/Yin_and_Yang/

Yin was described as feminine, black, soft, transformative, and providing spirit to all things. Yin may be represented by the color orange, although I consistently saw an ethereal milky purple. Yin must be symbolic for the second book, dedicated to Divine Mother, the feminine energy of the universe.

Yang was masculine, white, creative, strong, and provides form to all things. Yang may be represented by the color blue, and in the case of *Walking with Spirit,* the energy was definitely a deep blue.

Flying the Friendly Skies

I was flying with my family across the country. Not wanting to lose time, I typed my manuscript on the plane. Suddenly, we hit turbulence. I closed the laptop and closed my eyes. I wanted to pray to Archangel Michael to stop the choppy air currents in front of the plane. I have called on him to do this before and he has always come through and smoothed the ride. So, I prayed, "*Archangel Michael...*"

I heard, *"You are all right."*

I thought, *"I know."* As I thought the words, I discovered that I really did know. I rested my hands on the closed computer. My hands started to heat up and felt as they do when I am giving a Reiki healing to a client, hot and full of healing energy. I realized that while I was typing this manuscript, I intended to provide healing energy to the readers, and the words were actually infused with the healing powers of my guides. Awesome, that was precisely what I was hoping for!

My feelings of contentment were interrupted when our pilot spoke frantically over the loudspeaker. "Ladies and gentlemen, put your seatbelts on! We are about to experience severe turbulence for the next 10 minutes!" I thought that pilots weren't supposed to sound alarmed. I felt my heart rate quicken. I looked at my daughters who were looking at me. I closed my laptop and held on tightly, not sure what to expect. I closed my eyes and grounded my energy, and then grounded the energy of the plane.

Once again, I asked for Archangel Michael. I remembered that he had promised earlier in the flight that I would be fine. I heard him say, *"Do you believe in me or not?"*

I answered, *"Yes. "*

He said, *"Then keep writing."*

"But…" I started to protest.

I heard Michael's authoritative voice. *"Then keep writing."*

"Okay." I opened my eyes and opened my laptop. I wrote as if I didn't have a care in the world. A few minutes passed, and there had been no turbulence. Absolutely none. The seatbelt sign flashed off. My daughter looked at me and rolled her eyes. I smiled and thanked Archangel Michael.

And friends, that's how my relationship with my spiritual guides works. The archangels and Divine Mother present themselves as real to me.

chapter two

The Listening to Light Primer

This guide provides some definitions and fundamental concepts that will enable you to have a clear foundation for reading this book. For clarity in my writing, I show the question exactly as it was asked and include the yes/no answer in bolded print. All responses from Spirit are in bold italicized print. When there is a long conversation with Spirit, I have omitted quotation marks, so that you can feel like you are there with us, in the moment.

INCOMING MESSAGES

Typically, I receive information from Spirit during meditation or while working with clients. It is not unusual, though, for me to receive intuitive hits while I am busy going about my day. Sometimes I will be involved in an activity, and suddenly, I feel a heaviness in my throat or a fluttering in my heart chakra. I stop, tune into Spirit, and there is always a message or lesson for me. I find that no matter the source of the message, the information comes in through my senses. I have learned that the more open I am to listening and the more I acknowledge and value the messenger, the more often I am provided with information.

Throughout this book, I often use the word "see," but sometimes I hear, see, feel, sense, or suddenly know information. Often messages come to me through a combination of senses.

WALKING WITH SPIRIT DEFINED

I imagine that most readers perusing these chapters are pretty open to spirituality, so I might be preaching to the choir here. Several times throughout my life, I have spent time in prayer. But somehow, I never really felt like prayer was a two-way conversation. Maybe I was doing something wrong.

These past several years, I have experienced relationships with the Spiritual Divinity that I didn't even know were possible. In particular, I learned how to sit in God's presence, and communicated openly with the Divine Mother and Archangels. "Walking with Spirit" means consciously living in the physical realm, while frequently connecting to divinity in the spirit realm and being open to all that they want me to experience. Every day I check in with my guides, Divine Mother, and God, sometimes seeking guidance, sometimes seeking connection, and sometimes seeking their healing abilities. I check in with my guides every morning and try to stay open throughout the day; I never know what my day is going to look like or what the next lesson might be. Many days, I receive lessons by hearing, seeing, or feeling signs come in from the energetic realm. I love knowing that there is more to this life than what happens in the physical realm. Walking with Spirit really is about being in the moment, being in the here and now, and not trying to force a particular future.

I never thought a person in a body could have a connection to spirits in the spirit realm and live on two planes at once. At times it felt a little confusing, as though my head was in the clouds and my body was on Earth, but living in a dichotomy has gotten more natural for me. Walking with Spirit has many benefits and blessings. Not only is it a great comfort to me to have a connection with my guides, but I get information about the ethereal realm. All of this helps me in dealing with daily life in the physical realm and helps me keep life in perspective.

There is No "I" in TEAM

There is no "I" in TEAM. Or maybe there is, at least in this case. My part of serving on the team is being the sole member in a human body. I am the observer, the author, and the mouthpiece. I get the opportunity to confront my "I-ness," my fears, frailties, and flaws on a daily basis. I also get to use veto power, or say, "No" if something feels like it is not in alignment with my hopes, interests, or dreams. I am living with integrity and being authentic while walking with Spirit. I am not being coerced into doing anything I am not willing to do. My guides and I have agreed to move forward in specific directions so that this journey can unfold.

My team consists of Divine Mother, Archangels Michael, Gabriel, Raphael, Azrael, Cassiel, Uriel, and Metatron. We want to share the message that the Spiritual Divinity is within every person's grasp. They are here for us, each of them willing to provide profound love, wisdom, healing, and guidance.

My Other Half

If your perfect soul were in the form of a person, that would be your higher self. I first observed my higher self during a Reiki 2 course. During the Reiki attunement, a form of initiation via meditation, I took an energetic journey to a mountaintop and saw my higher self for the first time. She was tall, looked to be in her late twenties to mid-thirties with long, blonde, flowing curls. My higher self, later named Mi, (sounds like "Me") went to all the places instructed by my Reiki Master. At the end of the attunement, Mi entered a large field and was met by thousands of souls. I understood that I was now a member of this broader community of souls. I later learned that all these souls had a personal relationship with God or One Love.

Over time, I have seen that Mi is an amazing healer and teacher in the spiritual realm. While I am in my body, Mi does the work in Open Clinic that I wish I could be there to participate in. She speaks to and teaches other souls in the ethereal realm. I marvel at the connection she has with the divinity and at the things I have seen her do. The more I take actions and have conversations that are in alignment with my soul's purpose, the less difference I see between me in body and my higher self.

Open Clinic

I spend a lot of time in meditation. It was during meditation that I met my spiritual guides and the archangels. They showed me I could minister to souls who needed healing in the ethereal realm. This ministry was called "Divine Healing at Open Clinic." I was shown a place in the ethereal realm that was completely open and I knew there was going to be immense healing taking place there. I was told the name "Open Clinic," which made sense because souls could come and go. In my mind, it was open 24 hours a day, seven days a week. I later realized that in the spirit realm there is no such thing as "time" as we know it.

I became one with Mi, my higher self. I was ceremoniously appointed, and one of my spiritual guides gave me a minister's robe to wear while at Open Clinic. I watched while God's healing light came down, as if through the heavens, down through my crown, through my body, and out my arms and hands. I became a conduit of God's love and light. I saw that God's healing energy and light were holding space for healing in this vast arena.

I worked with Archangels Michael, Gabriel, Raphael, and the Divine Mother. At Open Clinic, souls came, and I saw the archangels and Divine Mother provide them grace, love, and healing. I learned intuitively how to read the stories that were taking place there. If I saw a gray energy mass, I knew that the soul had once been in a body and had passed away; the soul was still alive but no longer attached to a body. If I saw an energetic white mass, I knew that this was a soul that was there for healing and was still attached to a body in our physical realm. I was able to understand why each soul was there and whether they received spiritual, emotional, or physical healing. Once the souls received healing, they would return to their bodies in the physical realm or back to the Cathedral of Souls where they would reside until the next lifetime.

I thought Open Clinic was fascinating; I never knew what I would experience when I walked in. Sometimes there were just a handful of souls there for healing. Other times, I was told there were over a hundred thousand souls present.

Havingness & Knowingness

Havingness is a term that refers to a person's ability to accept something. For example, a woman who is incapable of keeping money in her pocket may feel she is not worthy of being secure and doesn't embody havingness for financial security. If this same woman wins the lottery, unless her havingness mindset is addressed, there is a good chance that all of the winnings will be spent in no time and she will soon be back to a place of living in lack. Our propensity for havingness is often based on the old stories we believe about ourselves, which can impact our relationships, finances, health, and amusement.

Knowingness refers to one's certainty about the truth of their beliefs. After years of being taught by Spirit, I have absolute knowingness that there is life after life and that archangels exist.

Divine Timing

Divine timing is the understanding that if something is not in accordance with the divine plan, it doesn't matter how much I push for it, it isn't going to happen. Sometimes, it all comes down to timing. I felt a great deal of relief when I finally understood the concept of divine timing. I was no longer trying to force things to happen. Life is much simpler this way.

In many cases, the stories in this book were written chronologically. By presenting them in this manner, I wanted to demonstrate how Spirit leaves hints or partial messages one day, and then in a day, week, or month builds upon the initial lessons. Sometimes it takes months or years before all of the pieces fall into place.

Learning Patience

There are people that I believe I am supposed to meet. Sometimes I get a vision that I am meeting that person, or sometimes when I hear or see a name, Spirit tells me I need to meet them. The other day my friend Denice and I were talking about our mutual friend Joe, and she brought up the name of one of Joe's friends. I heard loud and clear, "*Tell Joe to introduce you.*" So, I immediately texted Joe. Being in tune with Spirit, Joe said, "I know why you are supposed to meet them." I suppose I will find out why later.

Some of the folks I am supposed to meet need healing and I can assist with that, and others will help me carry out my calling: spreading the word that everyone can have a relationship with the Spiritual Divinity.

Some people I was supposed to assist came to me in spiritual form for healing, not in a physical body. Of course, I worked with them and facilitated healing. Does that mean that I will not be meeting them in person? That could be the case. I need to be ok with that possibility. Darn! I was excited about actually meeting and working with some of them. It has also happened that I was shown, without a shadow of a doubt, that I would meet a particular celebrity. I was having some angst about this future meeting, but I had so much divine guidance around this meeting, it seemed ungrateful for me to continue to question it. But what about free will? What if the person was hearing the call and choosing to exercise her free will and not follow what Spirit was suggesting? I would feel pretty stupid for publicly going out on a limb saying I knew I was supposed to meet her. What if connecting with her in the spiritual realm was all the meeting that I would ever have with her? Well, that has already happened several times, so maybe that was the introduction that I was told I would have. I needed to be ok with that, so I stopped plotting, planning, and worrying, and waited for Spirit and divine timing. So be it.

CARPOOLING

I was driving to meet with two of my intuitive friends, Caroline and Delphine. In the car, I was frustrated and agitated because I wanted to have all the answers to everything figured out now!

I felt an energetic presence; a male, middle-aged soul joined me in the car. He spoke. ***"Don't you understand divine timing?"***

"Yes, but I want a life-changing experience; I want to know more now!"

"Patience."

"Won't my impatience and desire to know more push things along more quickly?"

"No, it might slow it down more. It will come."

I saw a line of spirits in the spirit realm ready to teach me things and he spoke once more.

"When the time is right."

I checked in with my higher self, Mi. I asked, *"Is this a good guy to be listening to?"*

Mi was talking excitedly to others in spirit form. She looked at me, shrugged her shoulders and said, ***"I don't know who that is."*** Unimpressed, she continued talking with the others.

I laughed. *"Okay then, Mi, thanks!"*

When I caught up to Caroline and Delphine, I explained, "I think that my desire to know everything in the spiritual realm is blocking my spiritual life and ability to learn."

Reading my energy, Caroline saw that there was a boulder blocking my spiritual channel. She removed it energetically and got clarity on what was impeding my learning.

Delphine added, "You are very social on the spiritual realm. You are spending a lot of time in that realm and not in your body. You signed up for a physical experience. Your continued growth will come from you being in your body, not from being in the spirit realm. I see what I have seen before, that you do not want to come back in a body in a future life but want to stay as a spirit. I see that there is sadness in that. Your higher self is yelling NO! That is not what your contracts say. You are supposed to come back in a body for more learning."

Caroline continued reading my energy, "You are not fulfilling your contract with your husband and children when you are in the spirit realm so much."

Delphine concluded, "I see spirits lined up around you that you will be learning from, and spirits that you have written about in your book. They are the ones that are encouraging you to stay as a spirit and spend more time in the spirit world. You need to create more of a balance between your time in the spiritual and physical realms."

My friends helped me understand that pushing for continued learning, at the expense of time with my family, was going against the concept of divine timing. My learning about Spirit needed to be in tandem with being a mother and wife. Similar to the Yin Yang symbol, both parts were necessary for my personal equilibrium.

ASKING YES/NO QUESTIONS

While listening to Spirit, I have so many questions that I want to have answered. The best ways for me to get information is to interpret images that are shown to me or to ask yes/no questions.

One of the methods I use to get answers to a yes/no question is to do muscle testing. I create a closed loop with my right thumb and pointer finger and another circle with my left thumb and pointer finger. Interlocking the circles, I make a figure eight with my fingers. I ask a question that I know should be answered "yes," to create a baseline yes response. I might ask "Do I own dogs?" I test by pulling gently on my interconnected fingers to see if the link between the two links is weakened. If the answer to the question is affirmative, then the two links remain firmly connected, and I can't pull my fingers easily apart. Once I establish a yes baseline, then I ask a question where the answer is decidedly "no," such as, "Do I have red hair?" If the answer is no, there is a disruption to the link between the fingers, and my fingers pull apart easily.

I believe that the yes and no answers are coming from my energetic field and are specific to me. I have been told that when energy flows without dissonance, it flows freely in a circular motion without disruption, creating a closed system of continual loops. A yes answer to a question symbolizes truth or equilibrium to an energetic body; the closed system makes it difficult to break the linked fingers. If something happens to create dissonances, such as a falsehood or incorrect answer, the energy stops flowing freely, disrupting the closed circuit and allowing the connection between the fingers to be broken easily.

Not Everyone Will Get It

I had an uncomfortable situation awhile back. One of my loved ones sent my first book, *One Love: Divine Healing at Open Clinic*, to a family member that I knew would not be receptive to hearing about anything of an intuitive nature. I had no intention of sharing my book with this relative, but it happened anyway. This relative considers herself to be a devout Christian. She firmly believes that anything of an intuitive nature is of Satan, the devil, and should be vehemently avoided at all costs. She approached me, took both my hands into her own, and told me that she received my book. She said, "I just couldn't... just couldn't." She couldn't even finish the sentence. As if by even speaking about it out loud somehow relegated her to stand in the darkness with me. I said, "And you don't have to."

She reminded me that Christianity was based on God and salvation from Jesus Christ. I smiled and nodded as I am a firm and loving believer in God as well as the loving healing of Jesus Christ. We share the same values except for the area of intuition. She said that she would send me scriptures, no doubt to change my evil opinion on intuition, and that she would love to speak with me about it all later. I was more than happy to let the conversation rest. I have no doubt that if she had actually read my entire book, she would have understood that my love of the Divine is strengthened by working with God's healing light, Divine Mother, Archangels Michael, Raphael, and Gabriel, and Christ force, the loving healing energy of Jesus Christ. Not wanting to get defensive or try to change her mind, as that is not what I am here to do, I would be happy never to finish the conversation.

I have learned that my God is a God of love. God, as I see it, is an all loving God and does not alienate or isolate. I will continue to love my God, and she will continue to love hers. And it's all good. I know that she won't be the last person who tells me that from their religious viewpoint, my beliefs and actions are wrong. And I will know in my heart of hearts that what I have seen and experienced of God, the divinity, Divine Mother, and the angels is real. I would never assume that I know or understand the spiritual connection that someone else has in their heart or expect to understand how God is presenting itself to them.

Section One

The Divinity

ARCHANGEL CASSIEL

Cassiel means "speed of God," and is known for being associated with the seventh level of heaven. Archangel Cassiel changes his outward appearance to look like people of all different races and cultures; he represents all of humanity. Cassiel appears to me when he wants to support my efforts in sharing the message of The Ministry to the masses. Cassiel taught me that while we are individuals, we are all inextricably linked. What affects one of us impacts all of us.

ARCHANGEL AZRAEL

Archangel Azrael is the angel of death and is present at the moment of death for every person. Through meditation, he showed me what happens to a soul once it has left the body.

ARCHANGEL RAPHAEL

Archangel Raphael, whose name means "God heals," is also an archangel of Judaism, Christianity, and Islam. In the Christian tradition, Raphael is generally associated with the angel mentioned in the Gospel of John as stirring the water at the healing pool of Bethesda. Archangel Raphael is a very powerful healer and very masculine. He is a true teacher and has taken me on spiritual journeys through meditation to increase my knowledge as a student and healer. He is a protector of travelers, and he helps souls to transition after death. I have called on him for assistance with healing.

Archangel Metatron

My impressions of Archangel Metatron are that he is serious-minded and driven to make things happen quickly. I am grateful when he appears, and it is always accompanied by ideas for growth and expansion.

One day in meditation, Metatron appeared. I held my hand out to him. He showed me that he could warp time as we know it. He said, *"The constraints of time no longer hold you, no longer bind you."* Together we were in a black atmosphere with stars whooshing by at warp speed. Then they stopped, and I was floating in stillness, quiet. I felt a long, expansive "Ahhhhhhh."

Metatron said, **"Return and work from that place of ahhhhhhh. You will have all that you need. Just continue to move forward."**

Jesus Christ

I have long had a relationship with Jesus Christ, in both a traditional Christian relationship and now, in a working relationship with the loving, healing energy of Jesus Christ, known as Christ Force.

One time, when I was sitting with Christ during meditation, I received healing from him, and he was teaching me how to use healing abilities. I expressed doubts about whether I could use energetic healing or not.

He said, *"How can you doubt what God has given you to use?"*
Indeed, how can I?

God

I know everybody has their own terminology for the deity. Some people call it "Source," some people call it "the universe," but I call it "God."

What Keeps Us from Connecting with God?

One morning I went to Open Clinic, and there were many souls there that had passed on. I was trying to figure out why they were there, and I saw that each of them was there to seek healing in their relationship with God. I looked at them and I saw, if they had been in bodies, their 7th chakra would be blocked. When you are in a loving relationship with God, oftentimes, the seventh chakra is wide open. The crowns of their heads were blocked with energy, and I saw that there were two reasons that these souls did not have a relationship with God even though they really wanted one. The first was a pervasive and paralyzing sense of unworthiness, leaving them feeling unloved and unworthy of a connection with God. If I can't even love myself, how could God ever love me? This unworthiness created a separation between them and God.

The second reason was that some spirits had unrealistic expectations of God's role and purpose. Their unmet expectations led to hurt and anger and ultimately the feeling of being abandoned. The result was complete alienation from God or divinity. Their hostility towards God created such a barrier that they were not able to have a relationship with God. The energy was cleared, and they were able to experience God's divine love.

I have learned that God is a loving, energetic force. The God that I have seen loves us unconditionally and is always there for us but is not necessarily a God who performs miracles or gives us what we ask for, no matter how desperately we believe we need it.

One Love

As I learned new things, I began to question my understanding of God. The old constructs I was raised with no longer fit with the lessons I had learned.

During meditation in late February 2016, I was energetically escorted and taken up through our blue sky, out of our atmosphere, and into the black of the universe. I had no fear and knew that at any moment I could come back and ground myself. I was taken to experience an incredibly bright, white light, so white that mere words cannot describe it. I felt myself being healed emotionally, spiritually, and physically by an immense, extremely high vibrational healing energy. I was told that it was "One Love." I wanted desperately to understand more, but I was brought back to my physical plane. Each day I was shown and taught a little more.

I spent an entire month with Spirit teaching me about One Love. During meditation, I would float upwards and into One Love, escorted by Archangel Michael or Archangel Raphael. Each time I went, I was automatically very energized, yet at the same time, at peace. I felt such calm, unconditional love, and a sense that all was right in my body and the world. Frankly, there were times I just wanted to stay and not come back to the reality of my life in this physical world.

I was hungry to understand what I was experiencing. While with One Love, I felt like I was having my own personal communication with God. It must be God, because nothing else could be so all-encompassing, accepting, or loving.

I wanted to have words to describe it. I heard the words: "**One Planet. One God**." I wrestled with, but understood, that there indeed is only one God, regardless of the religious delineations and titles (Christian, Buddhist, Hindu, etc.) that people have created. I saw that all of the different religious groups that worship a loving God are gateway religions. They are all worshipping one power, one force, one God.

While God and One Love are interchangeable terms, I now think of the name "God" as it relates to humanity's understanding of and relationship to the deity. "One Love" is symbolic of the vibrational frequency described by Edgar Cayce when he wrote: "As is understood, Life-God-in its essence is Vibration." https://www.mcmillinmedia.com/sfg-1-resources-good-vibrations/

chapter four

Divine Mother

When I find myself in times of trouble Mother Mary comes to me
Speaking words of wisdom, let it be.
And in my hour of darkness she is standing right in front of me
Speaking words of wisdom, let it be.
The Beatles

People view Divine Mother in many ways. Some see her as Mother Mary, the mother of Jesus Christ. Others see her as Mother Nature, Mother Earth, or a divine feminine universal energy. I see her as a combination of all those descriptors. Divine Mother is the essence of all things compassion, nurturing, and maternal. Divine Mother encompasses nature, heaven, and earth. She personifies abundant grace and brings an all-embracing, all-consuming love to her healing.

Divine Mother has given me unconditional love and the impossible all-encompassing nurturing that my soul longs for in a mother.

Time spent with Divine Mother left me feeling intensely satisfied, wholeheartedly nurtured, wide open to love and be loved... very loved.

When I work with clients, I ask Divine Mother and Archangels Michael, Gabriel, and Raphael to connect with me and to provide guidance and healing on a spiritual, energetic, and physical basis. Lately, I have been noticing Divine Mother participating and emotionally connecting more with my clients. It seems that she shows up when someone I am working with, who is open to Spirit, needs nurturing, the nurturing that only a mother can provide. I watch as she lovingly wraps her arms around the person. Sometimes she has kissed them on the forehead or whispered in their ear. Her warm embrace was all consuming, and the clients reacted with such joy and contentment. In some cases, there was a thread of grief for what had been missing and desired for so long from their earthly mother.

I felt Divine Mother's presence at the Women's March in Denver. Her energy was palpable; I could feel her providing protection and support to the crowd of over 100,000 women and men gathered in support of women's issues.

At times, I have sensed the divine feminine holding space here in the earthly realm. "*Divine Mother, your nurturing Grace is outstandingly beautiful and welcome. Thank you for sharing your grace, your healing, and your compassion.*"

So, what is Divine Mother like for you? If you have not experienced Divine Mother before, I encourage you to open your heart, mind, and soul to spend time in prayer or meditation and invite her to sit with you.

Healing from Divine Mother

Sitting in meditation, I was embraced by the arms of the Divine Mother. I was being held so tightly that I felt her energy connecting with mine; I felt her healing me. The healing was focused on my heart chakra. I felt my heart chakra expanding as grief, and stuck energy that no longer served me were removed. The feelings were so profound that I wanted to share them, I want others to know how they can access this angelic love. I had been with Divine Mother before. But this time, as I was held in her arms, my eyes were drawn to something on her back. My hand reached out and I could feel feathers! All the times I worked alongside Divine Mother, I thought of her as being angelic and of spirit, but I had not noticed feathers before.

THE MANY FACES OF DIVINE MOTHER

When I get stumped in my understanding of the Divine Mother, I turn to my friend, soul sister, and expert on many things related to the feminine wisdom, Dr. Nancy Tarr Hart with Notre Dame of Maryland University. She currently serves as an Assistant Professor teaching courses in philosophy and religious studies. Nancy has a lifetime of connection with Divine Mother and has crafted her career learning and teaching about the feminine wisdom of the Spiritual Divinity.

I interviewed Sumaya O'Grady, a channel for the Divine Mother, on my radio podcast "Walking with Spirit" on the International Angels Network. The interview left me thinking about the many ways that Divine Mother presents herself to different people, so I phoned Nancy. She left me with a channeled piece of information.

Channeled from the Divine Mother through
Dr. Nancy Tarr Hart

"A reminder. We are not just one, nor have we only lived as one. We walk on Earth separately and together—individually and collectively, at different "times" and on different levels, and together. Quite often we walk separately but together...as a triad or not. Look to the Marys of ancient Israel for clarity. And to the triad goddess of old. Currently, I am present as a collective; you will find me with Wisdom at the gates of the cities, marching, standing with the Earth, the children, and between the me and the two. I am all of them together and apart. I am as I have been always".

I thought Nancy's information addressed my questions and reiterated the fact that I am not alone in my work and journey.

Nancy responded, "I believe absolutely you can interpret it in that way. But I think we're also being asked to see her presence (or her being present, as the case might be) in a multitude of earthly guises. Keep hearing where one or more of them are gathered in my name. But she has walked among us and continues to do so; either wholly or in essence."

I understood that people were so hungry to find glimpses of the divinity. I had grown accustomed to people seeing the image of Mother Mary in a cloud formation or in a burned piece of toast. But I hadn't understood the concept of the loving energy of the Divine Mother being expressed through acts of compassion, nurturing, or kindness through men, women, and children on Earth. As I have become more accustomed to working with Divine Mother, it has become easier for me to recognize her energy when it comes through someone in body.

The next morning, I sat with Divine Mother and asked more questions about my new understanding that she can present her energy through many different people.

Is that why different people see you differently?

Yes, but there is but one consciousness. Those acts are all loving, compassionate, full of grace.

Are there more faces of Divine Mother as times get more difficult here on Earth?

No.

Were there always these many faces of Divine Mother?

No.

Does the number of faces of Divine Mother change over time?

Yes.

Is my book representing one of the faces of Divine Mother?

Yes.

Thank you, I'm honored. Have I ever represented one of the faces of Divine Mother before?

Yes.

Have I represented one of the faces of Divine Mother while I was working with a client? **Yes.**

... while I was on my radio show?

Yes.

...when I adopted my daughters?

Yes.

Whenever anyone shows love and compassion are they showing one of the many faces of Divine Mother?

Yes.

When I think of the many faces of Divine Mother, I think about people seeing you or hearing you from the kindnesses shown to them. Is that what you mean by that?

Yes.

When people's acts of kindness or compassion are a result of your energy flowing through them, are they more God-like?

Yes.

When these people act, are they showing your compassion and love?

Yes.

Do people need to have a conscious knowledge that this is what they are doing?

No.

Seeing it this way makes love and compassion feel more like a viable force. Is love an energy?

Yes.

By concretizing love and giving it a shape and energy, will love be stronger?

Yes. See love, touch it, be love, and then hand it off to someone else. Make love palpable. Then do it again. Spread love throughout your day: in the grocery store, on the freeway, and in your work and homes.

Is love a life force?

No, but it makes living worthwhile.

Excerpts from "Not My Will but Thine"
Interview with Dr. Nancy Tarr Hart, Walking with Spirit Radio
Podcast, International Angels Network, August 16, 2018

Nancy: I look at Mary from a very physical perspective. But knowing also that she is part of the Divine Mother, the divine feminine actually too. I think that we see the Divine Mother or the divine feminine in many, many places; some of them are very unexpected. There is a big push to sort of separate out the Marys. For example, we have Mary Magdalene, and we have Mary, the mother of Jesus, and I think they were different people, but I think that they both have had that divine feminine working through them.

Ruth: That is something I wanted to ask you about tonight because you and I have spoken about the many faces of the Divine Mother. I have been shown by my guides that whenever someone is kind or doing something to help humanity, that that could be considered one of the faces of the Divine Mother. My guides told me that while

I am recording my radio show, writing my stories about the Spiritual Divinity, or working with clients to help them become their highest self, that I am showing one of the many faces of the Divine Mother.

Nancy, you had shared with me in a quick reading for me, that you mentioned my finding the many faces of Divine Mother; sometimes it's presented right next to me with a façade that is remarkably different than I might think. How can we recognize the many faces of the Divine Mother when we, I, run into it somewhere?

Nancy: I think that it's recognition of the energy. Let's say that there is a very wizened older woman sitting on a bench on a busy street corner who may look like maybe she is homeless. As we approach to sit on the bench because we are waiting for the bus, we may choose to either sit on the bench, or we may say, "I'll just sort of stand… or not." I personally would probably choose to sit because I talk to people. I talk to people in the supermarket. So, I would probably sit on the bench. And she looks over, and she just smiles. And with that smile, I would probably be able to sense through energetic feel; I tend to be very sentient, so I feel a lot. I see things too, but my strong sense really is feeling. And in my heart, in the area of my heart chakra, I would feel my heart blast open. And just be open to exchange that energy. And that's how I would recognize it; I think that we feel comfortable, we feel recognition, and sense recognition.

And, so I smile back at the lady, and I say, "How are you?" and she says, " I'm good; I'm better now that I've seen you." I can't tell you really how many times that has happened to me. And not necessarily an old lady, but people will say, "Oh, I'm sorry, I thought that I knew you, but it's really good to see you."

Ruth: That's how I felt when we first talked on the phone, like I've already known you.

Nancy: Right, and so I think part of that recognition, I think in our case, is two-fold. I think it was the divine feminine working through us. The other is that yes, our souls are connected, our souls are from that same tribe, that same grouping, and I think that we have been charged, not just you and I, we the people of the world, and in particular lightworkers, are being charged with continuing against what seems to be insurmountable odds. We are being asked to continue to do our best to keep those heart chakras open and to allow ourselves to be conduits and channels for that energy so that not only are people recognizing something in us that they will resonate to, either ask a question or just walk away saying, "Gosh, I feel better since I saw that person."

But we are also being asked to open that up so that more people can share in that energy whether they recognize it or not because it's also very healing. Because love is healing. That's what it is. And it resides in the heart. It's not in their minds. We like to think it's in our brains and our minds all the time, and that's what gets in our way. As I'm talking to you, my heart chakra is like pulsing.

Ruth: I know, I was just feeling that actually myself.

Nancy: I don't want to make it sound creepy or anything, but it's sort of the feeling that you get when you see small children laughing. And it just fills your heart with joy. Or you hear beautiful music or see somebody that you love.

Divine Mother, I think, works in very mysterious ways. Sometimes I think that Divine Mother appears as a man because I don't think that that energy knows any gender boundaries. So, energy is energy, and we are being asked to pay attention or be aware and allow. Allow it to flow through us because when we do that, we feel better.

We are better able to assist others, and it may change somebody's life. You most likely will change somebody's day. When was the last time that you said hi to somebody that you didn't even know and you know that they walked away smiling? And it may have totally changed their mind about something, or it may have changed the way they went about the rest of their day. And I think that is what we are here for.

Ruth: I just got a cool visual image of Divine Mother being a verb, like the energy of Divine Mother being a verb.

Nancy: That's interesting. Yes, an action verb.

Ruth: But thinking that it is something that you can do. Something you can emanate and be.

Nancy: Yes, that is my sense.

Ruth: Nancy, you talk about the energy of the love, kindness, and the compassion that comes through in all of the different variations of how Divine Mother is defined. Do you see that as similar to the love energy of God? Or do you see it as different? Are we talking about two separate energies here or combined?

Nancy: I think it emanates from the same source. Now, is it the same thing? I don't know. I think that we have been trying to figure that out for probably about 5,000 years, if not longer.

We are composed of some of the same energy that is in the stars. That energy is something that runs through us, and we are told in the Bible that God breathed into the first man to give that man life. He breathed into humanity, which implies that humanity has some of God, some of the divine source in it.

Ruth: It is interesting because here in the room that I am sitting, I can sense the energy of Divine Mother off to my left, and as you were speaking about, you know, is it God's love coming through her, is it different, is it the same, I'm sensing her saying, "It's God's love coming down through me." It's like I can see it coming down through her, but yet there is this mix, it's the essence of her that gets mixed into God's love, and then what we get is this even richer, delicious, feminine, nurturing, wisdom. It's just like rich.

chapter five

Nantucket Traditions

Nantucket
I sought validation here. I received it.
I sought tradition here. I created it.
I sought meaning here. I discovered it.
I sought connection to self here. I found it.
I sought connection to the Spiritual Divinity here.
They were waiting for me with open arms and hearts.
I learned how to walk with Spirit and then run with Spirit.
I found them all. Right here on Madaket Beach.

THE LOFT

My family has made a delightful tradition of spending a week on Nantucket, MA during the summer. As we take family and friends, it is cheaper for us to rent a home rather than several hotel rooms. I get the privilege of choosing the house we will be staying in. Sometimes I think Spirit is guiding me to pick a particular home.

One year, I found a home on Madaket Beach with our vacation dates available. The house had a loft bedroom that I quickly dubbed as my office. Each morning before my family arose, I climbed the ladder into the loft and meditated, anxious to see what Spirit was going to reveal. At the top of the ladder, I immediately felt Divine Mother and Archangels Michael, Gabriel, and Raphael. It was as if they were waiting for my arrival. The loft became a meeting room pregnant with potential. Each morning, my meditation time was rich with visual imagery and information from my guides.

One morning in my loft office in meditation I had a conversation with them all:

Here's how we want to change the world.

I'm ready.

You need to talk about Heaven and Hell. People need to know what that's about. The way will be cleared from above. There will be no barriers from above.

I saw an immense expanse of clouds from where I was sitting. All I could see were clouds to the right and left. Just clouds and blue sky.

What else should I talk about?

The angels. You see us. Talk about us. You know what we do, what we are capable of. People should know.

I thought of my humanness and limitations as a writer and speaker.

Don't compare yourself to others.

I had been thinking about Melanie Beckler and her strong platform of writing and speaking about the archangels. I hoped I could be as confident and well respected as she was.

Just go do. The Minister's license doesn't matter. You want that, so earn it. But for this work, it doesn't matter.

This house… this special house. Did you make this happen?

We will meet you wherever you go. The house doesn't matter.

Some houses, it just seems more like you are there. I thought it was this house.

No, some houses help you feel more open, accepting, amenable because the home has good intentions, and is light and spacious. It helps you to be more open. We are always there. It is a question of if you are open and ready or not. We always are. It is certainly easier when the surroundings are right. It is much harder for people who don't have these surroundings or living environments to be open, supple for awareness, and receiving. Here, there is not the need to transcend the environment to reach upward to the heavens and the angels.

Thank you that I have learned this about myself and that these opportunities can continue. I want to create my own income stream, so I can manifest these opportunities. Healings... I want to do more.

But that is one on one, and we want to go bigger. One on one is fine, but we can heal so many more if you get the word out.

How?

We will take care of that. You need to write. You get lost in the details of the business; just write. Elevate. Float in the clouds. That's where your words come from. Use this room and these sights as a guide and reminder.

I want to see Heaven.

Later.

My attention switched to the crashing waves outside the window.

This is where we want you to write from this week. We will give you the words.

Come Home to Nantucket

The following year we returned to the same Nantucket home. Once again, I claimed the loft as my unofficial office. I was excited to climb the stairs to see if the Spiritual Divinity were as readily accessible as they had been before. They were, and I loved it! The surf was pounding outside the window, and it felt like I had returned to a profound spot where earth and heaven come together to give me grace, inspiration, and divine connection. I exhaled. I was home.

Each morning I went to the loft to meet with my guides and spend time together. The archangels and Divine Mother were quick to meet with me. I received information as well as guidance on next steps. I felt I was being prepared to step further into the world to share their messages. Of course, I had no idea what that might look like or when.

My first morning back in the Madaket Beach house, I gathered my things and climbed into the loft. I sat on the bed and immediately felt my guides close by. I moved on the bed to face them. I needed to keep moving to change the direction I was facing because there were so many of them. I felt pain in my forehead and trance medium channels.

I said, *"Hello, let me clear my channels and run my energy."*

Divine Mother responded*, **"You don't have to do that."***

"I know." I was reminded that I did not need to do any of the protocol that had been taught me while I was learning about energy work.

I took stock of the divinity gathered around the bed. Divine Mother, Archangels Michael, Gabriel, Raphael, Uriel, Cassiel, Azrael, and St. Francis. It was like a Who's Who of the Spiritual Divinity. Christ joined us. It was everyone I have written about in my books.

I heard, ***"Keep writing. We are counting on you to keep writing."***

The following thoughts ran through my mind: animal communication, spirituality, energy, love letters, Christ's love, died for your sins, one way to Heaven, God's love came down through Christ.

My attention was drawn to a female being looking dreamily out the window to my far left. I decided to try to talk with her.

Who are you? Have I ever met you?

Yes that turned to **No.**

I was unclear of the answer, so I asked again.

Have I ever met you?

Yes that turned to **No.**

Hmmmm. Have I ever known your name?

No.

Have I felt your presence before?

No.

Have I seen you before?

No.

Are you an archangel?

Yes.

Are you female?

Yes.

Are you male?

Yes.

This was not surprising as many archangels have both male and female energy to them.

Do people know you by name?

No.

Can I know you by name?

No.

You are staring out at the ocean; I am assuming you have to do with nature or the cleanliness of the ocean. Do you have something to do with the ocean?

No.

If I keep guessing, will you tell me?

Yes turned to **No.**

Should I give up on talking with you?

No.

Are you here so I can learn from you?

No.

Are you here so I can tell others about you?

No.

Are you here because you hang out with all these other archangels?

No.

I was feeling resistance from the other archangels but didn't want to appear rude.

Are you here for a particular reason?

Yes.

Will I ever find out the reason that you are here?

No.

With all due respect, I am going to turn my attention to the other archangels. I am not turning my back on you, and if you want to tell me something, please let me know.

I turned my attention to the archangels in front of me. "*It is so fun to be back in this loft office with all of you!*" It felt like there was more animated talking among them. Perhaps I was able to sense them with more clarity due to a heightened awareness from the time I spent communicating with Spirit over the past year. I felt gratitude, respect, and thankful praise. I put my hands in a prayer position across my forehead like a Gassho position from Reiki.

Starting to my far right, I saw Archangel Gabriel. She said, **"Keep writing on your second book, Love Letters. It will come. Bring in the colors of love, the colors of Divine Mother, of love, and feminine energy."** I saw swirling colors of creativity: swirls of yellow, pink, orange, and green.

"I will help you."

"*Thank you.*"

Archangel Gabriel said, *"Blueberries. Pick each one; pick each word as if you were carefully choosing a basket of blueberries to create the perfect blueberry pie. The spices, the ingredients for the crust. Carefully mix the sugar; fold it carefully and with love for the person who is going to devour it hungrily. Nourish them like they never thought they could be nourished."*

"Will you help me?"

"I told you I would."

"I love that you used blueberry pie. It reminds me of my time with Sylvia in Maine. Those were some of my very favorite memories."

I worked my way around the semi-circle of archangels in front of me.

I came to Archangel Raphael. He said, *"We are there whether you believe in us or not, but you might as well believe in us because we can be really helpful to you. Remember all those places I took you to see during meditation? I can take others there as well. People can take me with them as they travel to remote places like mountain climbing and to places they are unfamiliar with. I have seen it all; your earthly realm is no challenge for me."*

I was reminded that the archangels are always available to work with us on earth.

I focused my attention on Archangel Michael. I saw my book *Walking with Spirit.* **"Focus on what you need to do to get it completed: editing, back of book blurb, reviews, etc. Make it the best it can be."**

I came to Divine Mother. My attention was drawn to all of the natural beauty that surrounds me here in Nantucket: the ocean, rain, greens of the grasses and trees, the smells, fireflies, sand, and waves.

"Oh, Divine Mother, that's why I love it here."

"That love that people hold for nature, that reverence, that appreciation that nature becomes a playground, a plaything... mountain climbing, challenging themselves to overcome what has been created for them to enjoy and appreciate."

"*Thank you, Divine Mother.*"

"Enjoy your family."

"*Thank you.*"

I continued around the semi-circle.

"*Archangel Uriel, why are you here?*"

"Because I am in your community now, and our work together is not finished."

"*Thank you.*"

I remembered that Uriel had given me a healing before. I felt pain in my trance medium channels. I remembered that I had forgotten to clear them but just started in talking with the divinity. Thinking of healings, am I getting a healing right now? May I have a healing? I yawned several times which was a symptom of energy moving. I felt pain in my back, which had been sore for about a week. "*Am I receiving healing in my back?*" I yawned again. "*Thank you for the healing. Uriel, is there more that you want me to know?*"

"Yes."

"*Do you do more than heal?*"

"Yes."

"*Do you want me to tell people that you do more than heal?*"

"Yes."

"*What else do you do?*"

"Educate."

"*Do you educate people?*"

"Yes."

I wondered if the book *Love Letters* should have more information about the different archangels. I asked my next question of the whole group. *Should the book have more about the archangels?*

I received yeses and nos.

"*Should the book have more about how folks can connect with the archangels?*"

Once again, I heard both yeses and nos.

"This is not working as I am getting too many opinions at once. Archangel Gabriel, should the book have more about the archangels?"

"Yes, no."

I tried to get clarification. *"Should the book have more about <u>some</u> of the archangels?"*

"Yes."

"Should the book have more about how people can connect with the archangels?"

I heard both yes and no. *"Should the book have more about how people can connect with <u>some</u> of the archangels?"*

"Yes."

"Archangel Michael, should the book have more about you?"

"No."

"Archangel Raphael, should the book have more about you?"

"No."

"Divine Mother, this book is dedicated to you. Should the book be only about you?"

"No."

My attention was drawn to her left. I saw Christ.

"I understand that you would like me to include more about Christ. I hadn't thought about the book being so much about Christ."

Divine Mother replied, **"Well, that was the ultimate love letter, the ultimate sacrifice. Christ coming down as a human and losing his life out of love for others."**

"Archangel Uriel, do you have anything else to add?" All of the archangels appeared humbled and quiet. Clearly, Christ held seniority over the archangels.

I heard a chorus of nos.

"Thank you for the healing, Archangel Uriel!"

"Archangel Cassiel, I have not heard from you." I saw all of humanity and remembered that was what Cassiel represented.

"Write for every man. Write such that every person can connect with and be fed by this book. Bring Christ to every person."

Divine Mother ended our session. *"Now, go be with your family, paint, and have fun!"*

IF A TREE FALLS...

The next day was wrought with technological difficulties. Yes, we were on an island in the Atlantic Ocean, but Wi-Fi and cellular data were readily available. So how was it that I could not get any forms of telecommunications to work for me, while no one else in my household had any difficulties?

I texted, sent emails, and even tried to make a phone call that was cut off within the first few minutes. How is it that all attempts to reach out that day were thwarted? Sometimes when it seems that someone or something doesn't want my words, my message, to connect or be heard, technology in all its forms fail me. But that encourages me to keep trying even harder.

If no one answers, does that mean I didn't reach out? Exasperated, I gave up.

When words fail me, I finally give up, and I go inward. What can I hear, see, assimilate, sense? In order to receive information, I need to be silent, still. I need just to be.

I closed my eyes, and I immediately saw Archangel Michael.

"We are always here. Stay true to you. Stay true to us and the vision."

BE A BEACON

In meditation, I was joined by Archangel Michael, Divine Mother, Archangel Gabriel, and Archangel Cassiel.

"You are a beacon; don't get caught up in the lower level energies of this realm. A beacon or lighthouse doesn't get dimmed by the wars going on around it; it keeps shining regardless. Remove all doubt and fear and any stumbling blocks. Remove all frets of human insecurity and ineptness."

"What are my journey and purpose?"

"To illuminate the world about the possible connections with archangels and Divine Mother."

Archangel Cassiel spoke next, **"The world needs you."**

"Do they really?"

"Yes."

"But how do I tell them?"

"Radio."

I thought of the message I was trying to put out into the world: how to connect with the Spiritual Divinity.

"Why is that my platform?"

"Because you are not alone and that has brought great comfort to you."

"How do I push out to make my light shine brighter?" I used my arms to push clouds away from what I imagined to be my beacon. I must have looked like I was swimming. I needed to clear lower level energies and concerns from the space around my light and I needed to clear out any beings that had infiltrated my space to constrict my energies or limit my reach to others.

chapter six

The Divinity in the Loft

I meditated in my loft office and was immediately joined by Arch-angel Michael, Divine Mother, Archangel Gabriel, and Archangel Francie, a guide for my finances. All of the guides felt warm and welcoming except for Divine Mother. I tried to find out what was wrong.

I feel like you are unhappy with me and have been for a few days, like a disapproving mother.

I feel like you are trying to make money off of my name.

I am trying to teach others about you. I do need money to be able to do this. Yes, I would like to make money for freedoms and travel but not travel for travel's sake. I love to travel to feel more connected to Spirit.

I had a vision of Nelson Mandela, and the strength of Spirit he gained while incarcerated.

True, some people learn all they need to learn about Spirit while in jail, but I want to learn more from seeing different places and experiencing different things.

It sounded as if I was convincing myself that my wants were acceptable.

I have free will to want what I want.

You don't know the real me.

Her statement surprised me.

Okay, please teach me. This book is written for and about you.

I don't want it; not this way.

Please forgive me for whatever I did to displease you. Please show me what I did to displease you.

You don't know love. You can't write about love if you yourself do not experience it. I watch you with your husband and children. You ignore them and leave them to do for themselves, leaving them feeling like you aren't there for them. You have become absorbed in your writing. Isn't that the exact same thing that hurt you about your father?

I was humbled.

Yes.

They need to know that you truly love them, that you would trade life for them, that you are the one truly safe place to call home.

I do love them very much.

Your husband doesn't know that, and your daughters need more. There will always be work and books to write, but there won't always be these three to love.

But, I want to milk every minute of rich connection with you all while I am here in Nantucket. My connection to you all feels richer here.

Then don't write about me.

Ouch. That's fair. Thank you.

I closed the laptop and went downstairs to spend the rest of the day with my family.

Two Fathers of Christ

As a special treat, my youngest daughter and I spent the night in the loft. It was fun getting to spend time together doing something adventurous. The window behind me was open; I could hear the crashing of the surf and feel the cool breeze. Through my immense appreciation of the ocean during meditation, I experienced a deep cleansing of energy. It was a beautiful way to start my morning.

In my loft office, I meditated and was met by Divine Mother and Jesus. Before sitting with them, I grounded my energy, even though they told me in the past that I didn't need to.

Divine Mother said, *"The reason that we let you do these things is that you are pure in heart and you are trying to teach others."* I think she was referring to grounding my energy, but I was not sure.

She continued, *"I want you to teach others that loving Christ is the most important thing. That his love is pure, and that people can know God's love by loving Christ. God sent his son that mankind could relate to a man; a person they could see that carried both man's and God's characteristics. When he said, 'I am in the world but not of the world,' a phrase that you yourself have felt and used, he was saying that his heart and spirit related more to the ethereal realm."*

I was curious. *"How did Jesus see God? As a human shape or as an energy source?"*

I was allowed to see and feel God from the vantage point of Jesus. I experienced an immense, white, very bright, loving energy. It was familiar energy to me, just as I had witnessed God's energy before.

"This is how God feels for me. Wouldn't he feel different to you, his son?"

Jesus said, **"He is father God to everyone, no matter who comes to him."**

I reflected on God being energy and not in the shape of a man. Just energy.

"As his son, did you want him to take on the shape of a man?"

Jesus said, **"Why? I had a father. Joseph of Nazareth."**

"Can we just sit in God's presence together?"

As Jesus and I sat in God's presence, I noticed that God's light did shine differently on Christ. Of course, I thought so! God does favor his son! As I was observing the difference, I saw that Christ knew how to relate to the strong energy better than I did and so the energy was more concentrated with him.

"So, the better one is at receiving God's love, the more they can receive?"

"Yes."

"How can I get better at receiving?"

"Open your heart and your mind and relax. Cast out all your worries and thoughts of the world, your children, your home. Everyone needs to find their own connection to God. Don't put your children, husband, or your belongings into the mix of your connection to God."

I consciously pushed aside all thoughts to simply be an open conduit or vessel in preparation for feeling God's love. As much as I have sat in God's presence before, I realized that I was holding onto pain in my heart that I was putting before this moment of sitting in grace with God.

Like a huge, old, dead fish, I flung the pain in my heart at the feet of God. It symbolized my father's passing. I didn't realize I was holding onto grief. I missed him. Watching him die was so hard. I felt like I should have done better or more for him the night he passed, although I couldn't think of what I could have done differently. That look Dad gave me the night he passed was filled with such love and gratitude. I knew he loved me, and he knew I loved him and was there for him.

Jesus said, **"That love you had for, you have, for your father, I have that same love for mine."**

"Joseph?"

"Yes."

"How is your love for God different than my love for God?"

"I have two fathers. One that I learned the ways of the world from: how to live with men, about life in the world, how to be a man, how to play fair, have a trade, love a woman. I was human after all."

"How was it different with God as your other father?" I asked.

"Through God, I learned how to pray, how to fast and care nothing for the earthly pleasures while sitting in what you call meditation, to talk with my Godly father."

Jesus continued, **"There were dark times."** I saw Jesus sitting alone under very dark gray clouds praying and talking, pleading with God about what was going to be happening to him in body. I heard Christ pleading with God, **"Why do I have to go through this? I know why. I don't want to go through this."**

God answered, **"I know. You know our plan."**

Jesus said, **"I know. But what if it isn't worth it? What if my dying doesn't make a difference for mankind?"**

God responded, **"It will make a difference for some. Your story will matter to some, and they will learn through you. Their hearts will be open to loving you, and ultimately to loving me. Their individual hearts will shine as beacons in the darkness and will enable others to see the light. The more who are illuminating the light of God, the more love, and brighter and lighter the hearts of others."**

The Holy Spirit

During this conversation with God, I saw what I thought of as energy. I thought that if one person's energy was lighter and brighter, and another person saw that, they would wonder why their energies differed. They would ask about what they had noticed and would want that for themselves. Soon the brighter and lighter energy would impact more and more people, making the world a more harmonious place. I decided to ask the Spiritual Divinity about my ideas.

Is that what it's like?

NO! I am talking about people loving God! Not wanting to be "brighter and lighter."

Okay, understood.

This is about loving God! A personal loving connection with God! That's all that matters.

Wait a minute, I didn't recognize the voice.

I don't know who said that.

The voice was coming from the direction of Divine Mother and Archangel Michael.

Who is talking to me?

It seemed like I needed to do a roll call.

Divine Mother?

No.

I knew that.

Jesus?

No.

Right.

Archangel Michael?

No.

I heard the words "**Holy Spirit.**" I thought of what the Bible refers to as the Holy Ghost or Holy Spirit.

Holy Spirit?

Yes.

Have you spoken to me at other times?

Yes.

Then, welcome back! When I say I am talking with Spirit but don't know which spirit, am I always speaking with you?

No.

Sometimes when I am talking with Spirit, am I speaking with you?

Yes.

I heard the words, **"Listening to Spirit."**

I liked the phrase, "listening to Spirit," as it had a different feel than "walking with Spirit." My thoughts returned to the Holy Spirit's vehement reaction to my description of energy. I wondered where I had erred.

Loving God is only loving God. It is not walking in a higher vibrational frequency. While that will help others to feel better and make the world a better place to live, because people will be treating each other with more dignity and respect, it is not the same as loving God. Love God with all your heart and soul.

What is that phrase?

I remembered it from the Bible. While I quote some of the verses, I also reject some of it as man-made doctrine.

They didn't get it all wrong.

I detected mild sarcasm.

Talk to me about the Bible.

Love God, know and love Christ, love your fellow man. When you love your fellow man, you will not do the things the Bible says to not do, like lie, cheat, steal, or kill. It boils down to love God, love Christ, love man. All there is, is love. God is love.

I was reminded that I need to learn more about love.

Holy Spirit, will you talk with me?

Yes.

Have you been with me since I was a child?

Yes.

Have you been with everybody since they were a child?

No.

Were you with me because I already knew Christ?

No.

Were you with me because I was going to know Christ?

No.

I felt my energetic connection to the Holy Spirit get weaker.

Holy Spirit, will you answer a question?

No.

Archangel Michael, will you answer a question?

Yes.

Do all archangels know the Holy Spirit?

Yes.

Can you answer all my questions about the Holy Spirit?

Yes. Learn what you can about the Holy Spirit.

Is the Holy Spirit energy?

Yes.

Is the Holy Spirit with everyone automatically?

No.

Does the Holy Spirit have to be asked in?

Yes.

Did I ever ask for the Holy Spirit?

Yes.

Did I do that before I was born?

No.

Did I do that when I accepted Christ as my personal lord and savior at age 13?

No.

Did I do that before then?

Yes.

Did I request the Holy Spirit knowing that was what I was doing?

No.

Holy Spirit, thank you for listening when I asked you to be with me.

I continued my conversation with Archangel Michael.

Does the Holy Spirit always enter when someone asks?
Yes.

When a person asks Jesus Christ to be a personal lord and savior, does the Holy Spirit automatically come with it?
Yes.

Can the Holy Spirit come to a person without coming through Christ?
Yes.

*When I heard, "**Look left** " so I wouldn't get in a car accident, was that the Holy Spirit?*
Yes.

Is the Holy Spirit God?
No.

Is the Holy Spirit a gift from God?
Yes.

I found it intriguing that while I could now recognize the voice of the Holy Spirit, I still had no picture or feelings associated with its presence.

Section Two

Light

chapter seven

Energy and Light

I chose to sleep in the loft, again, but this time not for the adventure. I wanted to wake up early, connect with my guides, and get working on my manuscript.

I was met by Divine Mother, Archangel Michael, and Archangel Gabriel. My attention was drawn to a woman in spirit who was looking out the window at the ocean. Was she the spirit of someone who had a previous life on Nantucket?

Once again, I sensed that Divine Mother was frustrated with me. I wondered if anyone else has ever experienced an angry Divine Mother? I have never read about anyone feeling the displeasure of her before. I must really be out of line somehow. I cleared the space between Divine Mother and me, thinking that maybe there was a being or stuck energy impacting how I perceived her. I was able to clear a being, and in so doing, the anger and displeasure was lifted. But then I observed her not as angry, but sad. I understood that she was sad that it was taking me too long to get the word into the world telling people how to connect with the Spiritual Divinity. True, last year in this same loft office, Divine Mother asked me to speak out about my relationship with her and the archangels. I had done that some on my radio shows and written about it in articles. But my second book *Walking with Spirit* was coming out 15 months after she asked me to write about it. Here I was working on a third book, and while Spirit had been sharing a great deal of information in Nantucket to include in this manuscript, I still had no idea what the completed book would look like. I didn't even have the title yet. I had been given a timeline that it will be completely written before the end of August. I responded with, *"Well, then I need help to see the format and outline."*

Divine Mother turned toward me, **"You are lying in bed. You should be writing."**

True, I was sitting in the bed with my back propped against the wall while I typed what was being said to me. I wouldn't say that I was lying down. How odd that I would be feeling defensive with the Divine Mother.

I countered with, *"Well, let's just get on with it then."* This was actually what I had been longing for since we had arrived in Nantucket: concentrated time to work on this manuscript in the presence of my guides.

Archangel Gabriel stepped forward rubbing her hands together like she eagerly anticipated helping me. We started discussing the book right away.

You see the topics, help me to organize them.

I had made several false starts in the past few weeks and had a running list of the topics I thought might be included.

Love, connection, healing, grief, death.

Can I write about raising vibrational levels of energy?

No.

Can I write about energy?

No.

Can I write about light?

Yes.

Can I write to help raise someone's levels of light?

Yes.

In hindsight, I understood why Divine Mother presented herself as being upset. It was the only way I could understand that something was amiss. Had she continued being her pleasant, loving self, I would have missed the point entirely.

Thank you, Divine Mother.

I wanted Archangel Gabriel to explain the difference between energy and light from a spiritual viewpoint.

Light is of God. Light is God's gift, God's love. God connects to man through light.

Spiritually speaking, is there any correlation between energy and light?

No.

But God created energy, right? Did God create energy?

Yes.

Life force.

Is energy a life force?

Yes.

Is love a life force?

No.

I suppose you could survive without it.

Is light a life force?

No.

Is a "life force" something that is required to have life?

Yes. While energy is a life force, God's light is a gift.

Energy just exists. Energy is everywhere.

When we talk about light, are we talking about the light of the sun?
No.
I knew that. I just had to ask for clarification.
I heard the words ***"Let there be light."*** Of course, I was reminded of the first words in the Bible.

In the beginning God created the heavens and the earth. Now the earth was formless and empty, darkness was over the surface of the deep, and the Spirit of God was hovering over the waters.
And God said, "Let there be light," and there was light. God saw that the light was good, and he separated the light from the darkness. God called the light "day," and the darkness he called "night." And there was evening, and there was morning—the first day. -Genesis 1:1-5, New International Version

But this is about the sun. And you told me that spiritually, light refers to other than the light from the sun. I think it must be a metaphor for something else, like God's love and connection to man.
I looked online and read: The reality of the creative power of God's voice has important spiritual implications that go well beyond the creation account itself. Light is often used as a metaphor in the Bible, and the word "illumination" (meaning "divine enlightenment of the human heart with truth") has to do with bringing things into the light. Spiritual illumination is a kind of "creation" that occurs in a human heart. "God, who said, 'Let light shine out of darkness,' made his light shine in our hearts to give us the light of the knowledge of God's glory displayed in the face of Christ." (2 Corinthians 4:6). https://www.got-questions.org/let-there-be-light.html
So, is it ok to write about raising someone's light?
Yes.

Does the word light refer to trying to become more godlike?

Yes.

So, when I am trying to help people raise their levels of light, I am trying to help them become more like God?

Yes.

Are you going to teach me more about light now?

Yes.

Then you have to help me.

I saw swirls of purple and rainbow colors.

Are there different colors associated with varying levels of light?

Yes.

I saw a vision of a rainbow.

Why am I seeing this? Are the colors of the rainbow associated with different energetic frequencies?

Yes.

Do the different levels of light relate to the different levels of Heaven?

Yes.

That was all the time we had. I had no idea where this line of thinking would be leading me, but I figured I would eventually be shown.

Getting to Know Divine Mother

The next morning, I was meditating and noticed that I had been joined by Divine Mother, Archangels Michael, Gabriel, and Cassiel. This was a smaller, more intimate group than I am used to working with, so I was a little surprised at who had and hadn't shown up.

I wondered what emotions Divine Mother would be showing me. Recently I had seen her be sad, loving, compassionate, and at times even demanding. I wasn't sure how to prepare myself for what might be coming up.

After a minute, Divine Mother started a conversation.

There is so much about me that you don't know.

Why do pictures always show you as one dimensional?

Because they don't know me. You are taking the time to get to know me. I am female; I have emotions.

I thought of what Divine Mother represents to me: the divine mother of Christ. She was a person in human form. Of course, she would have had emotions. Plenty of them. Did those emotions follow her into the spiritual realm when she left her body?

As a spirit, do you have a full range of emotions?

Yes.

As I am sitting here with you, do you represent Mother Nature?

Yes.

Mother Nature is not always smiling, serene and calm. We have storms, hurricanes, tornadoes, and volcanoes.

Can those things ascribe to the term "fury?"

Yes.

Does Mother Nature get angry?

Yes.

I saw a vision of rain.

Does Mother Nature ever get sad?

Yes.

Is Mother Nature energy?

Yes.

Is Mother Nature an energy?

No.

As I am sitting here with you, do you represent Mother Nature?

Yes.

As I am sitting here with you, do you represent the mother of Christ?

Yes.

As I am sitting here with you, do you represent the universal feminine energy?

Yes.

I wondered if the muscle testing I was using to receive answers just represented what I thought to be true, or what was actually true. I was reminded that muscle testing had shown me things in the past that I had no understanding of or belief in, before that moment in time.

What do you want people to know about you?

The love of a mother. I can be that for those who have not experienced that. Even for those who have a mother who they love, I can still love them like a mother. I provide, and they can feel loving compassion and nurturing. If men felt this love, there would be less fighting and wars. People who are content do not need to fight others to get what they feel is rightfully theirs, because they are not lacking anything.

Stars

I had a vision of the light emanating from stars as they shine at night. I know for me, stars have represented a connection to others. The first 40 years of my life, I would look up at the stars and feel a longing for someone I loved but didn't know. It was odd, and I didn't have a construct in my mind to attach it to, to help it make sense to me. In my 30s, the longing became greater and at times brought me to tears. In my early 40s, I adopted two daughters from China. I realized after they were home in America that when I looked at the stars, I no longer had the same sense of longing. It felt like a contract had been completed and that which I had longed for all these years was finally with me in person. I wanted to talk with Divine Mother about stars and light.

Can we get back to talking about light? Do stars have a spiritual significance?

Yes. You are getting off track.

Okay, what else do you want me to share about you?

The vision of the stars persisted, even with Divine Mother's admonishment. Apparently, if someone is willing to listen, the Spiritual Divinity have a lot to share. I felt a sense of loving connection emanating from the stars, available to anyone looking up at them. The love felt connected to God.

Did God give us the stars?

Yes.

The voice speaking to me seemed different, suddenly.

Who is speaking to me? Divine Mother?

No.

Archangel Michael?

No.

Holy Spirit?

Yes.

God gave you the stars to bring light into the darkness. The stars are a symbol of God's love for you. Some people use them as a reminder of loved ones who have passed before them.

Can we get back to the rainbow?

No.

Are we still discussing stars?

Yes. The stars are a directional compass and were used by shepherds in their fields at night. Now, they are more romanticized.

I have always loved stars.

You have always been a romantic.

I know.

I was reminded of the stars on the crown that I was given at my ordination at Open Clinic.

In spirit, Skip came to me and put a minister's black robe on me. I was honored, humbled, and amazed. Then he approached me with a crown of shining stars and went to put it on my head. I was immediately uncomfortable with the thought of being exalted and said, "No! I can't do that!" All of my religious upbringings had focused on worshipping only God, never a person. I would not wear a crown that could make it look like I was trying to be Christ-like. He responded with, "This isn't about you! This is about God, and how He will heal through you!" Embarrassed, I understood. My role in Open Clinic as a healer was to have God's grace and healing come through me to the souls; I would be nothing more than a conduit. I could do that! From *One Love: Divine Healing at Open Clinic Author: Ruth Anderson*, SageHouse Press.

I remember thinking at the time that it was odd that the crown I had been given had stars on it, yet it reminded me of Christ's crown when his was a crown of thorns.

Was my crown symbolizing that I was a conduit of God's healing light?

Yes.

Guiltily, I thought of all the time I had not consciously been in Open Clinic over the past several months.

I have not risen to the task of the gift that was bestowed on me.

That's right.

But Mi is there, right?

Yes.

chapter eight

We Have Plans for You

I felt like Divine Mother, in the form of Mother Mary, was very disappointed in me and had been for several days. I wondered if my friend Nancy Tarr Hart ever felt like she disappointed Divine Mother? I know that Nancy has a personal relationship with her. Did Jesus Christ ever disappoint his mother? What did it feel like when he disappointed her? Did it feel like this?

I was stubbornly holding onto my life on Earth and the things I enjoyed doing; I had enough time to do both my work and that of the Spiritual Divinity. Did Divine Mother have a purpose for me that I was not aware of? I decided to ask her.

Divine Mother, do you have plans for me?

Yes.

Do you have a purpose for me that I am not aware of?

Yes.

Do I have free will to accept it or not?

Yes.

Will you be disappointed in me if I don't choose it?

No.

Yet, you are disappointed in me now, when I am not doing what you wish for.

Yes.

I am choosing to not focus on the fact that you are disappointed in me right now.

We both smiled.

Am I at least on the right track for your plan for me to be revealed?

Yes.

Do I need to ask you for your plan for me to be revealed?

Yes.

Does your plan for me have to do with life here on Earth?

Yes.

Does your plan for me have to do with the spiritual realm?

Yes.

Is your plan for me a life of service?

Yes/No.

Is your plan for me a life of educating others?

Yes.

I thought maybe I was unique because Divine Mother had a plan for me.

Do you have plans for other people?

Yes.

Okay, then I'm not special at all.

Archangel Michael, do you have plans for me?

Yes.

Are they the same plans that Mother Mary has for me?

Yes.

Archangel Michael, do you have plans for other people as well?

No.

Archangel Gabriel, do you have plans for me?

Yes.

Do you have plans for all other people?

No.

Are your plans for me the same as Divine Mother's?

No.

I smiled wearily. How could I possibly entertain competing interests from the Spiritual Divinity regarding how I spent my time on earth? Archangel Gabriel showed me a future vision of many books that I will have written, if I continue with her guidance.

A lyric from the Hamilton song, *Non-Stop* ran through my mind; a line that I had sung to myself several times, as I saw myself in the words:

Why do you write like you're running out of time?
Write day and night like you're running out of time?
How do you write like tomorrow won't arrive?
How do you write like you need it to survive?

I have devoted copious hours to my work in the past five years, more than I ever did in my earthly career, and I was a workaholic at that point. Maybe I am so obsessed with my writing and my newfound passion because I am trying to fit in my life plan with those that Divine Mother and Archangel Gabriel also hold for me, not even aware that is what I have been doing. At the same time, I don't want to lose myself in the process, my interests or my desires, while focusing so much on writing.

THE COLOR OF CONNECTION

I wanted to learn more about my vision of the rainbow. I brought it up again with the Spiritual Divinity.

Now, can we talk about the rainbow?

Yes.

Is there more to the light and rainbow than I previously learned?

Yes.

Is the rainbow a gift from God?

No.

Is the rainbow simply light and water?

Yes.

I thought of Noah's' Ark and how I grew up believing that the rainbow was a sign from God.

Was there really a Noah's Ark?

Yes.

Was the rainbow a sign from God then?

No.

Okay, that just ruined everything I learned in Sunday School as a child.

I smiled.

So, stars are a gift from God?

Yes.

I wasn't sure what to do with that, so I moved on.

So, what did you want me to know about levels of light? Do the colors of the rainbow relate to God?

No.

Who am I talking with? Divine Mother?

No.

Holy Spirit?

Yes.

You said I could talk about people raising their levels of light, right?
Yes.

I saw a vision of the rainbow colors I had seen previously and was given questions to ask.

Is there a color of the rainbow associated with people?
Yes.

Is there a color of the rainbow that has to do with the spiritual knowledge of people?
Yes.

You said that the different levels of light relate to the different levels of Heaven. Do the rainbow colors have to do with the levels of energy in heaven?
No.

Do the rainbow colors have to do with the spiritual knowledge of souls in Heaven?
Yes.

Can the same be said for on Earth?
Yes.

I needed to take a few minutes and let that sink in.

Wow, interesting! Do the colors stay in the same order as on the rainbow?
Yes.

I reviewed the colors of the rainbow. The order is red, orange, yellow, green, blue, indigo, and violet.

Are souls with the most spiritual knowingess the color red?
No.

Are souls with the most spiritual knowingess violet?
Yes.

I thought of the people called "indigo children," who have a high level of spiritual understanding. That makes sense. I saw the colors of the chakras. Red symbolizes the first chakra, which has heavier, denser properties. I saw the numbers 1-7 moving upward, each number associated with one of with the colors of the rainbow. They moved upward from red, to orange, yellow, green, blue, indigo, and violet, which represented higher and lighter properties, an openness to God and consciousness. I suddenly saw how all of these things fit together.

Can you classify people's connections to God using colors related to the rainbow?

Yes.

Do the levels of the Cathedral of Souls fall into alignment with the rainbow colors?

No.

Okay, I get it now.

While I can't use color to sort the levels of the Cathedral of Souls, I can use color to classify each soul's connection to God?

Yes.

Are the souls in Level Seven, otherwise known as Hell, red?

Yes.

Do the souls in the levels move up in accordance with the chakra colored scale?

Yes.

So, are the souls in level six orange?

Yes.

The souls in level five are yellow?

Yes.

The souls in level four are green?

Yes.

Are the souls in level three blue?

Yes.

Are the souls in level two indigo?

Yes.

Are the souls in level one violet?

Yes.

Is this the same for on Earth?

Yes.

Is there a benefit to having this knowledge?

Yes.

Hmmmm. I wasn't sure what the benefit was.

Does this color scale represent anything more than knowledge of Spirit?

Yes.

What? Does it represent morality?

Yes.

Does it represent the love of God?

Yes.

Does it represent service to others?

Yes.

Does it represent one's love of mankind?

No.

Interesting, why not? I associate love of God and acts of service with love of humanity. Are they interrelated?

No. It is true that many people who love God and who do acts of service also have a love of mankind.

But what about, "Love your brother as yourself?"

It's not that that isn't important. It is that which is asked of you. But it isn't looked at for these ratings.

Are these color rankings really just for my work?

No.

I can't fathom that God is ranking souls by colors either in the physical or spiritual realms. Is God ranking souls based on colors?

No.

Are the angels using this color ranking?

Yes.

Are the archangels using this color ranking?

Yes.

Is this so they know who to work with?

Yes.

Is this so they know who to answer?

Yes.

Is there anything else?

Yes. Light, go back to the topic of light.

I saw a prism, the colors of the rainbow. The colors green and purple stood out to me; purples being those most connected to spirit, and greens being smack in the middle of the spectrum.

That's who you want to focus on.

I want to focus on the purple ones?

Yes.

And the greens?

Yes.

The purples are already connected with Spirit. Are lightworkers purple?

Yes.

Why would I focus on lightworkers?

To bolster them and help them to stay strong when times get difficult. The world needs them to stay strong and be at the ready.

Why would I focus on greens?

Don't focus on the reds, because they are closed off. They have too much growth to go through and you will not be able to reach them.

Okay.

Blues and indigos are well on their way, and they don't need you. They might enjoy what you are saying and feel connected to it, but they aren't the ones who really need it.

Okay. How do I reach green people?

They don't understand Spirit, but they are not closed off to it. Start

with what they know, like nature. Hook them in with writing what they know, then show them that Spirit is connected through nature. Then you can take them and stretch their reach. Stars. Write of stars and your love and heart connection to the stars. Everyone sees stars.

Who am I talking with? Archangel Michael?

No.

Holy Spirit?

No.

Divine Mother?

No.

Archangel Gabriel?

No.

Archangel Cassiel?

Yes.

That makes sense as you symbolize how to reach humanity. Thank you. Can I do that with this next book?

Yes.

Archangel Cassiel, will you help me?

I am helping you now.

I smiled, but he didn't.

Right.

Archangel Gabriel, will you help me to write?

She smiled.

Yes

What was there to learn other than what I already understood about the levels of energetic frequencies and behavior? I was reminded that this new learning was about light and not energy, a distinction that was obviously important to the Divinity. For my purposes here, light is an important concept, but energy is not.

chapter nine

The Ultimate Love Letter

My morning session in my loft office included only Divine Mother, Archangel Michael, Archangel Gabriel, and Archangel Cassiel. It was an intimate gathering.

Divine Mother showed me her son, Jesus, on the cross. I saw dark, overcast, angry skies when Christ was killed. I saw Divine Mother screaming and crying.

I don't want that to have been in vain. People don't know about him anymore and are lost. They are living with no compass, lives of greed, malice, contempt for the God who made them and loves them. Are you writing this?

I smiled.

Yes, Divine Mother.

I felt her pleading.

I need you to listen. Tell them that we are here, that Christ loves them and can help them; that he was once a man like them. I lost my son to appease mankind. They didn't believe he was who he truly was: the son of God.

Divine Mother wept and cried out.

Hear me! Oh Lord, why don't they hear?

She turned to me.

Man is destroying themselves, their hearts, the earth. Tell them. Tell them, but not with anger, with love. They need to know that there is love for them here.

She gestured to the archangels.

We can guide them, show them, teach them. That is what I want from you. Your plan that we spoke about earlier, for you to lead hearts to Christ, to love Christ.

I saw a vision of Heaven in the afterlife, the top level of the Cathedral of Souls, and how each of the levels 2-7 paled in comparison to the top one.

Heaven. Yes, Ma'am, that's where I want to be.

Then earn your place.

How?

By teaching others about it, about Christ, about his love.

I fidgeted, yawned, wanting to change conversations to other learnings.

See? Even you change the topic.

Sorry, do you have more for me?

Yes, more hearts need to turn to Christ, so his death wasn't in vain.

But some people have turned to him. How many hearts need to turn so you don't feel his life was in vain?

As many as possible. All of them.

I turned my attention to Archangel Michael.

Anything?

He deferred to Divine Mother, his respect apparent. I saw the color apricot and felt and saw the earth. Is this the color and feel that the world could be if there were more Christ-loving people in it? No, the feel of the apricot world was not warm or caring. I saw how easily apricot could turn into red and was reminded of the colors associated with the souls of people. Red was the lowest color, representing the least evolved connections to spirit, morality, love of God, and service to others. Is apricot the state of the world right now? Are there some people who are pulling the rest of the world up to a higher level?

Warrior for God

During this same meditation time, I asked," *Who am I connecting with? Divine Mother?*"

A voice said, **"No."**

I really wanted to know who I was talking with. *"Archangel Michael?"*

"No."

"Holy Spirit?"

"Yes/No."

I kept trying. *"Who is talking to me? Archangel Cassiel?"*

"No."

I felt Metatron's presence. *"Archangel Metatron, are you talking with me?"*

"No."

I felt Archangel Uriel join us. Yikes! All of my heavy hitters were there.

"Archangel Raphael, are you here?" I asked.

"Yes."

Tears came to my eyes. All of these archangels there with me at once; this was big. I took a deep breath. I was so humbled to be among this group.

I heard many voices from the archangels together in agreement. ***"Rise up! You need to stand tall. We have prepared you for this, for this work. You don't get to stay small. The world needs you."***

"Ok, what?" I asked.

"The world is nearing its destruction. Politicians are playing a shell game with your lives. The hearts of men need to know, women and children need to know that times will be rough, but we are here for them. Tell them."

Archangel Metatron stood huge, bringing tears to my eyes and taking my breath away. He showed me how to make myself taller, massive, to match his size and gain more power. I rose up over the Divine Mother and archangels. My body shuddered as I released the stuck energy that was in my way, holding me back. I saw that I was girded with the armor of the warrior angels I had seen months ago: a sword, shield, and body armor on my chest, and knees.

I came back down to average size, still in full protection. *"Thank you, Archangel Metatron for showing me that."* How do I reconcile this warrior of Spirituality with me, the woman who shops around Nantucket buying chocolate covered cranberries with my children?

My attention went to Archangel Uriel. Am I going to receive gifts from each of my guides to better stand in my truth and take on this journey? Uriel reminded me of the healing powers he first showed me when we met. Here in the loft, I received healing that was yellow-apricot in color to my third and second chakras. The healing of my third chakra was to embolden my sense of self and self-esteem. The healing to my second chakra was for me to have more compassion and empathy for others, to be able to see others for who they truly are, and for the struggles that they walk through.

"Thank you, Archangel Uriel. Can I use this healing energy with others?"

He answered, ***"It is not energy; it is light."***

"*Okay, I think I appreciate the differences between energy and light now. Archangel Uriel, can I use it in my work?*"

"**Yes,**" he replied.

"*I have received strength, might, healing light... what else?*" I asked the group of angels.

Archangel Gabriel smiled. "**Creativity, cunningness,**" she replied. I watched Gabriel infuse my brain with a dusting of green and gold glitter.

Archangel Cassiel got my attention. He said, "**Every man.**" I saw a slideshow of the different faces of humanity, playing across his face. It then was moved into my heart, helping my heart be open to assisting every man, woman, and child.

"*But how?*" I asked.

"**Not now. That will come.**"

Next up was Archangel Raphael, representing safety for travelers. "**I will be with you.**"

"*Where am I going? Thank you for being with me,*" I responded. I saw a vision of Paul the disciple in Corinth and saw that Archangel Raphael was with him at that time.

I noticed someone else near me.

"*Archangel Francie, is that you?*" I asked.

"**Yes, there is a reason I am here with you. You will have what you need.**"

I felt as if I was being prepared for a mission trip, but I didn't know where I was heading.

Next, my attention was drawn to the female being who had been looking out the window. I had been told she was an archangel, but who was she? I thought she had been sorrowfully looking out to sea, but then I asked, "*Is she looking out the window as a sentry?*"

"**No.**"

I tried talking directly to her. "*Are you an archangel?*"

"No," she answered. Unsure, I turned to Archangel Michael.

"Should I be listening to her?" I asked him.

"Yes." I wanted to know more.

"Archangel Michael, is she an archangel?"

"Yes/no."

"Does she represent sorrow?"

"Yes/no."

Then, I understood that she was once human and had worked her way up to being an angel. Checking my facts, I asked, *"Was she once human?"*

"Yes. As a human she loved the ocean."

I got the feeling that she was not as high in stature as the archangels or Divine Mother. I smiled. *"Congratulations!"* Good for her for working her way up to get to work with the archangels!

"Does she have a name?" I turned my attention to her and asked, *"What should I call you?"*

I heard, **"Sarah."**

"Can I call you Sarah?"

"Yes," she answered.

I turned back to Archangel Michael.

"Why is Sarah here?"

"For companionship. This can feel like a lonely journey, and she has been through that. As an angel who was once human, she understands. You can talk to her."

"Thank you and welcome!" I said to Sarah.

I turned to Divine Mother. She said, **"God bless you; you listened."** Mother to mother, I felt her love of her child, as only another mother would understand. I took this to mean that she was asking me to help make her son's death on the cross not in vain.

"I love you, Divine Mother."

"I love you, child," she smiled.

Lastly, I faced Archangel Michael. He said, "**I will be with you. This is still The Ministry and Open Clinic, but instead of souls coming to us, now we are going to them.**"

"*Okay, but I still have a family that I am committed to spending time with. Okay, bring it on, but I want to get this book completed.*"

ANDREW

The next morning, I climbed the ladder to the loft for time with my guides. The same guides were here as yesterday, and I sensed a new being directly to the right of me. It presented as orange, yellow, and brown, like reedy foliage in the fall. I saw strips or reeds of color, not obscure fuzzy colors, but a combination of individual strands of color.

Thinking about the colors and feel of the field of reeds, I thought of fall. I felt bittersweet emotions from my memories of a time when there was more vibrant life, and a longing for something that had passed.

The presence came into my energetic space. It felt like nature, but nature by itself would not necessarily impose its presence on me.

I asked, "*Why are you in my space?*"

The presence continued pushing its way into my personal space. I turned to face it and moved backward in body to get out of its way. When I faced it head-on, it bowled me over with its energy. I put my arms up to block it, and Archangel Michael laughed as if my attempts were futile.

I backed up further and got to a place where I could sense its energetic boundaries. The reedy strands were no longer multicolored, but merely yellow. Even Archangel Metatron, who typically presents much larger than the other archangels, was smaller in stature today while this new being made its presence known.

Archangel Michael, is this an Archangel?

Yes.

Does it have a name?
Yes.
Is it a common name?
Yes.
Will this being be important to me on my journey?
Yes.
Is it male?
Yes.
Female? Although the energy felt predominantly male.
Yes.
I put my hand up to read its energetic and light properties.
Can I read its energy?
Yes.
Can I read its light?
Yes.
Is it a healing archangel?
Yes.
Does it heal on a physical basis?
Yes.
Emotional?
Yes.
Spiritual?
Yes.
Has it been to Open Clinic?
No.
Have I met it before?
No.
Archangel Michael, did you arrange for me to meet this Archangel?
No.
Did the Holy Spirit want me to meet this archangel?
Yes.

Does this archangel work with the other archangels?
Yes/No.
I took that to mean that it works with some of the archangels.
Archangel Michael? Does it work with you?
No.
Divine Mother, does it work with you?
Yes.
Archangel Gabriel?
No.
Archangel Metatron?
No.
Divine Mother, did you want me to know this archangel?
Yes.
Did this archangel use to be human?
Yes.

I remembered what I heard before about souls in the Cathedral of Souls being able to work their way up to angel and archangel status.

Did this archangel in human form know Christ?
Yes.

I saw a vision of a dusty road; the dust being kicked by sandaled men.

Does this archangel hold the memories of Christ while on earth?
Yes.

I realized I was being given access to this spiritual being so I could ask questions and get answers about Christ from someone who was with him. Awesome!

Divine Mother, you are so funny.

She definitely wanted me to write about Christ and orchestrated this meeting. Maybe I would use this for a future book.

Was this archangel one of the disciples?
Yes.

Wow! I was humbled and honored to have this opportunity! But his invasive method of introduction wasn't welcome or appreciated.

Why did you present so large and in my space? It felt very obtrusive to me.

As a man, I had a large, strong demeanor. I had to learn to command my ego.

I rolled my eyes. Perhaps the lesson had not been thoroughly mastered.

I believe that I knew Christ in a past life. Did I know you?

Yes.

I remembered a vision I had been given of following Christ to share his messages with others; I had been an information sharer, like what would be a newspaper reporter of those times. I saw a larger male push me away from Christ's side as if I was insignificant. I sensed that this man was Andrew.

Were you gruff with me?

No.

I saw me, a smaller male being moved aside. I reframed the question to work with his ego.

Was I in your way?

Yes.

I thought his response was ego-based.

You thought you were pretty significant being one of Jesus's disciples.

I just wanted to be near him. I wanted to hear all that he said.

If I ask your name will you tell me?

Later.

I heard "Andrew" from the other Archangels as if they were unimpressed with his attitude of self-importance.

Are you Andrew?

Yes/No.

Was your name Andrew when you were alive on earth?

Yes.

Do you go by a different name as an archangel?

Yes.

Can I call you Andrew?

Yes.

Can I channel you for a future book?

Yes.

Divine Mother, is that what you want of me?

Yes.

Is there anything else?

Write your book and get it out there.

Archangel Gabriel, will you help me and give me some direction?

Yes!

I saw her jumping up and down excitedly.

WALK ON MADAKET

My niece and I took a long walk around the tip of Madaket Beach. Our adventure covered four miles and three hours, and we noticed only a handful of people. We saw many forms of marine life, some dead but most alive. We luxuriated in stopping to take photos and marvel at the sights, sounds, and smells. As we walked and talked, it became clear to me that this time was a journey of the heart and the soul. Spirit was using this time to heal, and gift me by feeding my soul.

The color of the ocean water was pine green, giving it an old-timey feeling. The frothy white waves reminded me of white antique lace. A seagull flew overhead casting a shadow on the white foam. The sand was various shades of rich brown. I thought of how far I had come as a spiritual being in the three years since I last photographed shadows of gulls on the sand in Madaket.

I wanted to take a photo of a shadow of a gull on the white waves with brown sand and dark green waves. I waited for a gull to fly over-head so I could catch the scene on film. I told Amanda that I knew the perfect photo would happen, but it might require patience and a few minutes wait. As I waited, happily soaking in the colors, sights, and sounds, it felt like I was receiving a total package of healing through Christ's love to mind, spirit, and body. The visuals coming together produced healing to my fourth (heart) chakra, which is represented by the color green. Several gulls flew overhead, but their shadows were cast on the dune and not on the beach.

I jokingly asked the gulls to move a little to the left, so they would be in perfect alignment for my photo. After a few minutes, a seagull flew right over the water. It was in line to get the photo I wanted. I got the photo. As I reviewed the photo later, I saw that the seagull, shadow, green water, white foam, and brown sand all made it into the photo. It was perfection!

I thought of the photos I took three years earlier, with all of the same elements included except for the seagull. I thought, of course, in the same way that I could only see Spirit's shadow back then, I can see Spirit much more completely now. Of course, I should have a photo of the source providing the shadow. I had come a long way!

We walked around the tip of Madaket beach where the waters con-verge, where I saw past life memories on the trip the previous year. About 9 or 10 seagulls sat on the beach in a close grouping. I stopped short and stared. The sun glistened brilliantly on the upper outline of their wings, and I thought that they looked somehow angelic. It felt like their appearance was a gift, as if each of the gulls symbolized someone who was there for me in spirit form. My thoughts turned to the archangels. I felt a genuine connection between body, soul, mind, and heart. As we approached, the seagulls took flight. The dazzling white continued shining on the top of their wings as they flew off.

Ocean Healing

Morning time in my loft office was sacred. Sitting on the bed in meditation, I found the same guides as yesterday, including Andrew. Our time together the past few days had been very rich. While I had written everything down, I had not had time to assimilate much of it.

I think my brain is full.

Hold on; empty it.

I smiled.

Just listen.

I saw green foliage swaying in the breeze, cattails on a lake down the street from my childhood home. As a child, my older brother and I spent hours trying to scoop minnows, tadpoles, and fish into buckets. I would break apart the soft, brown skins of cattails and send the fuzz flying in the breeze.

You have always had a love of nature; a connection to your soul by being outside. You feel it, that connection with nature. Nature feeds your soul. It's here for you to enjoy.

I saw fish, bugs, and my joy in talking to them. I felt their energy.

Had I been connecting to the spirits of these living things?

Yes.

I remembered the walk I shared on the beach the day before, and the seal that I talked to that made me smile. I saw the two seals that came by afterward. The first felt like it was very wise. It was dark black, had deep penetrating eyes, and it surfaced four or five times as it passed. I felt like it had connected with Amanda and me energetically. I had spoken with it as if it could hear and understand what I was saying. The second seal was a much lighter brown, smaller, and had youthful energy, like a teenager. It popped its head out of the water, and it felt like it had a spirit of amusement and adventure to it. I would have sworn it was laughing at us because it startled and surprised us when it surfaced.

The walk; everything you saw was a gift, filled with treasures of nature: the horseshoe crabs, the dark green water, bright white lacy foam, seagull shadows, and their flying close to you. You felt healing to your heart chakra. The seashells, algae, even the dead mother seal and her dead baby nearby told you a tale of love and devotion. That deeply felt connection to nature is available to you any time.

On our walk we had come across a thin, newly deceased female seal and her baby a little further back on shore. the baby looked bloated as if it had been dead longer. Neither had obvious signs of foul play or physical assault. I asked Divine Mother to show me what had happened to them. I saw darkness lit by moonlight.

Was it at night?

Yes.

Did the mother die first and the baby stayed with her?

No.

Did the baby pass away first and the mother stayed with it?

Yes.

Then she got beached?

Yes.

Did the mother get beached on purpose to stay with the baby?

Yes.

Was the baby a boy?

Yes.

I tested my previous answer.

Was the baby seal a girl?

No.

That was so sad.

Thank you, Divine Mother.

Okay, folks, is there anything else?

No. Wait, yes.

It was Divine Mother.

I love you. Thank you for caring about the seals.

chapter ten

Listening to Light

The word "Listen" contains the same letters as the word "Silent."
-Alfred Brendel

While spending time listening to the many archangels and Divine Mother, I was given a new name for this book: *Listening to Light*. I ruminated on the dichotomy of two very different senses. Hearing and seeing. Listening and light. I asked my guides for more insight into the title.

What does "listening to light" mean? What does "light" mean in spiritual terms?
The Divine.
And what about the word, "Listen?"

Silence in meditation. Hearing, feeling, sensing, seeing. It is not enough just to take notice, but to listen and interact as well.

Archangel Uriel, are there things I still need to learn about light?

Yes. A man's soul can be seen in terms of light.

I thought of light in terms of brighter or dimmer. I wanted to check that I understood what I had been told earlier.

Can you also see souls in terms of color?

Yes.

I used what I had learned before to formulate my next question.

Can colors be used to identify a soul?

Yes.

Is that similar in the earthly realm as well as in the Cathedral of Souls?

Yes.

Do different colors of souls separate themselves and hang out on different levels?

No.

Why not?

Because the greatest growth and change come when there is a sharing of ideas or philosophies; there is a synergy in the free-flowing exchange of ideas. Souls can learn from each other. If you want to keep people from learning and growing, keep them in groups of others exactly like themselves.

Archangel Uriel, is there more for me to learn?

Yes. These are two different things; the white divine healing light of God is different than the colored lights of human souls.

Should souls try to become more like the light of God?

No. No one can ever become like God; only God is God. Man should not try to be God. Man can try to be God-like in thought, mind, deed, with love in one's heart for mankind, and doing acts of service for others. But man can never become God.

Archangel Uriel, when people say that they are God, what is your interpretation of that?

That is man deluding himself. No one is God.
Can someone say that they are of God?
What does that mean?
I don't know; that God is in them?
Then why not just say that God is in them?
Good point.

With my eyes closed, I saw God's light above me and to my left. Below that and to my right was a vibrant rainbow. I sat looking at God's divine light. In the lower, right-hand corner, I saw a faded image of a rainbow.

Is that a reflection of the rainbow below it?
No.
Is there a rainbow in God's divine healing light?
Yes.
Why?

Looking at it, it was a straight strip of rainbow colors, not arched like a rainbow, and it was upside down with the purple at the top and red at the bottom.

What does it symbolize?
It symbolizes God's love for man. And that God made man and man is of God.
Oh, so man is of God!
Right. God would like to be recognized as such, to be in a loving connection with individual people.
So, when people say that they hate God, they hate the father who created them, who is an integral piece of them?
Right.

As I looked at the ribbon of rainbow colors, I noticed that the purple and indigo were more diffused colors, as God's divine light was penetrating through. As the colors worked down to red, the color was more solid with little or no divine light passing through. I thought of the colors of the souls represented by the rainbow.

Archangel Uriel, seeing the divine light seeping through the purple and indigo, does that mean that God is working through them more than the lower colors?

Yes/no.

Does it mean that the purple and indigo souls are more open to God's energy?

Yes.

Archangel Uriel, do you have anything else for me?

No.

Divine Mother?

No.

Archangel Michael?

Yes.

Archangel Gabriel?

Yes, I will help you.

Archangel Michael, what else?

I saw an image of Christ and the rainbow.

Was Christ here to love and be open to working with everyone, regardless of what color their soul was represented by?

Yes.

Was there one group or color that Christ was more focused on?

No.

Is there anything else?

Yes. Christ.

I saw him on the cross.

He died on the cross for you.

I know that; on a profound level, I do.

LEAVING NANTUCKET

In preparation for the morning we were to leave Nantucket, I set my alarm, so I could have quiet time with my guides. I stayed up late playing cards with my daughters and relished writing into the early hours of the morning from my loft sanctuary. When the alarm sounded, I fought unsuccessfully to stay awake. Minutes later, I was gently awakened by a large, rose-colored light that filled the room and my mind; I knew right away it was from Divine Mother. The glow was warm, loving, and enticed me to waken fully. I walked to the far side of the loft where I met daily with my guides. I sat and identified each guide. They were spread throughout the room in a semicircle around me. Every guide I spent time with the past two weeks was in attendance except for Archangel Andrew.

In spirit, I saw myself dressed as a warrior angel and knew that our time together would include a great deal of symbolism for my upcoming work. I meditated and immediately began shifting energy, which I reminded myself was to increase my light as a spiritual being. I hoped and wondered if I would be given a blessing from my guides for protection, guidance, and inspiration as our retreat in Nantucket was coming to a close.

I watched as a column of light shone from my body reaching upward as if toward the heavens. Typically, a column of light would be coming down from God, but this time it was emanating up and away from me. As the column of white light moved upward, it opened up to spread all around me. I saw me as the beacon, but now I had a brighter, taller, more expansive reach of glowing light around me. I cleared what I initially thought was stuck energy but then realized that I was clearing my light. I had never cleared my light before, only my energy, and wasn't sure how to do it on my own.

"Can people clear their light?" I asked.

"Yes, but we will save that learning for another day."

My mind wandered to how I could teach others to clear their light; perhaps I could end my private sessions with clients that way. Then I heard and felt nothing from my guides.

I needed to reconnect. *"Wait, what's happening?"*

"You will need to learn to listen even more carefully to us now," they answered.

I understood that the work we would be doing together was becoming more complex.

They continued, *"Your listening these past few days was good. We are talking about people's souls. That is a huge responsibility. You will be leading others to the light."*

"I have nothing set up to be doing that. What written material, website, books, or radio shows I have in place are inadequate," I protested.

"No, not like that."

I saw a vision of myself, guiding people through the dark toward the light in spirit form.

"Don't focus on the 'tangible how'; focus on the intent."

In body, my back was aching, so I changed how I was sitting and propped my back against the wall. I no longer directly faced Archangel Michael or Divine Mother, but other lesser archangels. I felt a distance between us and communication between us stopped. I turned back to face Divine Mother and Archangel Michael.

"Keep your gaze on us. We are your compass through this journey," they advised.

My weekly radio show came to my mind.

"After classes on Divine Mother, teach about Archangel Michael. Introduce each of the archangels on the show."

"Like a 'Meet the Archangels' series. Which archangels should I include?"

"Metatron, Uriel, Gabriel, and Cassiel. Include a meditation."

"So, listeners can invite each one of them in and feel their presence."
I felt the rose-colored light around me again.

"Come back to the circle, back to this place of love, for guidance, when you need to be nourished."

The rose light turned to red, and I was bathed in rich, red light. I knew this healing was enabling me to be more comfortable around others from all energy levels. Archangel Azrael came to mind, and how he dealt equally with both the lower level energies and the higher level energies. I was very quickly immersed in each of the other rainbow colors of light, not one at a time but all at once.

A large sword appeared in front of me.

"This sword of truth is for you to discern the truth when choosing guests [for the radio program]. **Only have teachers on who are in alignment with your truths and not speaking to feed their egos."**

I then received a shield plate on my chest, covering my heart.

"Guard your heart that no one can come in and change your heart or the purpose of your work."

I saw a vision of shoes symbolizing my long journey ahead, both traveling back home and as a teacher and healer. I envisioned being back again on Madaket Beach and in this loft office.

"Thank you, I want to come back. It feels like home."

"It is home because we are all here with you. We will all be with you anywhere. This is not your only home."

I was surrounded in green light. I wondered if it symbolized money, as we had discussed it several times recently.

I hadn't formed a question, but I heard, **"You will have what you need."**

The green light turned to yellow, and I felt healing in my third chakra, signifying my center of self and self-esteem.

"You have the strength of self to face whatever you encounter."

The yellow light became blue, triggering and providing healing to my fifth chakra, which represents my communication space.

"You have the words and can communicate eloquently. Don't ever think that you don't."

My laptop pinged showing me that my friend Linda emailed wishing me safe travels. Was she referring to my flight home or on this spiritual journey? As she is my soul sister, I smiled and assumed both.

Divine Mother bathed me in a bath of purple loving light. This was followed by being immersed in God's divine healing white light.

All of a sudden, it seemed like the pace of our gathering was speeding up. It was as if there was a rush of trying to get things done promptly, but I wasn't sure why.

Divine Mother, the archangels, and Sarah having been in a semicircle around me, came even closer. They each put a hand on my shoulders and head in a "laying on of hands" to bless my work and signifying that they will be there to support me. Tears of love and gratitude came to my eyes. I turned and looked at each one, thanking them for being with me on this journey.

My cell phone alarm went off, disrupting the quiet and signifying that it was time to head to the airport. I think the blessing and goodbye at the end was rushed because everyone, except for me, was aware that my alarm was going off any minute.

I silenced the alarm and turned my attention back to my guides. I expected them all to be there still, but they were gone except for Archangel Michael and Divine Mother. I wasn't surprised that they were the last two standing at my side.

Section Three

Healing

chapter eleven

Grief

*Scars don't make you a broken person,
it means you have successfully survived.*
- Author Unknown

Some of us hide our scars, while others define themselves by their scars. In the long run, we are all defined by our life experiences; whether we perceive them as character building or life-shattering is up to each of us individually.

LIVING IN COLOR

One day, my friends gave me an energetic healing. As they connected with my spirit guides, they described what they were seeing. Delphine spoke of my grief over my father's illness and preparation for his passing. Caroline saw my intense relationship with spirituality and that that was where I was seeking my comfort. Hilary saw that I had been living my life in isolation and void of connection, life, or color; everything was in black and white. They saw my body hanging on a cross in respect, devotion, and connection to Christ. I was surrounded by serious, devout energy and was very comfortable staying there. They lovingly showed me that continuing to live in pervasive grief and fear was not in my best interest. In the meantime, I had been missing out on connecting with my husband or daughters for months. I hadn't been allowing anyone into my emotional space.

Energetically, my daughters entered and showed how they missed spending fun times together. Indeed, I had been lost in my thoughts, nurturing my emotions, feeling my pain. How could anyone expect me to be having fun while I was mourning the upcoming loss of my father? It would seem sacrilegious to be silly at this time. Somehow, I thought if I was enjoying life I was being disrespectful to my father and unappreciative of what he was going through.

Caroline started laughing. Energetically she was shown my daughters grabbing handfuls of colored paint and throwing them onto the image of my white body on the cross. I responded, "You can't throw colors on me; I'm on the cross, and this is serious business!" My daughters laughed and persisted. They surrounded me with love, perhaps equal to or greater than the love that I feared would be lost with my father's passing. My daughters used this love to fill holes that I had in my emotions and heart and chakras. Slowly, the color was allowed back into my life, and I saw that it was not only okay, but better for me. Living in color would not diminish the love I have for my father; it would not lessen the pain I would feel when he passed. I saw the importance of living in the present. It finally made sense to me that I could honor my daughters and the love that we share, enjoy them in the here and now, even while experiencing grief. These two emotions do not need to be mutually exclusive. Thank you, Caroline, Hilary, and

Delphine, for the gift of love and for giving color, connection, and joy back to my life.

I have been personally touched by several older friends and family members contemplating their upcoming transitions. In conversation with each one, it is not the pain of living these experiences that they talk about. It is the love they shared with others over the course of their lives that has touched them the most deeply. May each of us feel loved, really loved, by someone today. And conversely, may each of us love, really love, someone today.

Divine Timing in Death

During his last few hours of life, I prayed that my father would die. I was horrified by the thoughts running through my head. Dad repeatedly said that he wanted to go, and at least twice had asked my sister and me to end his suffering. He spoke with a macabre tone, which made me think if we had the implements he had requested, he would have let us use them. He managed a laugh when I told him I loved him but would not go to jail on his behalf. Watching his body working so hard at shutting down was excruciating. I was acutely aware of the concept of divine timing. Until it was his soul's time to check out of his body, it wasn't his time yet.

If I accepted the idea that the time of his death was predetermined, then that time just hadn't happened yet. If I went with the idea that something needed to happen before he could exit, then maybe that thing hadn't happened or was in the process of happening. Who knows what was happening in his heart or in the hearts of others he had touched? Maybe forgiveness and healing were rolling out somewhere that I was not privy to. I was aware, however, that my sister and I got the validation we needed from our father during the last several hours of his life. Maybe that is what his soul was waiting for.

If you have a loved one who is holding on past what makes sense physically, perhaps the best thing you can do to be helpful is hold space in love and light. And know that divine timing will eventually come to pass.

The Clipboard

When I learned about souls that were part human and part otherworldly, I had mixed feelings. My first reaction was that they must have lower level frequencies, be void of the ability to connect, and be lacking a conscience. Then I asked about my pre-life makeup and was told that I, myself, was a combination of human/alien/angel. So, I am one of "them." Great. I wasn't sure what all that meant, but it was stretching everything I thought I believed.

As I wrestled with that possibility, I had an epiphany about my father. All of my life, his focus was on his research first, and then my mother. The fact that they had four kids barely created any disruption to his life plan. Speaking for myself, most of the time I was in his presence, I worked hard to be invisible. My formative years were instrumental in creating a mantra that served me well at home, and later at work. It was "Duck and Cover."

My father was brilliant. Throughout his career, he amassed a total of 53 patents. I was in awe. His focus on research consumed his life until the day before he passed away at 88 years of age. Every spare moment, he sat in a reclining chair with his clipboard in hand, his latest research held protectively under the silver metal clip. Much of the time it looked like he was lost in thought. I have since come to realize that my father was in the zone of meditation, connecting to his ethereal connections, and receiving scientific guidance.

The idea that my father could be human/alien made complete sense to me. His off-the-charts intelligence, struggles to connect emotionally, and ability to get downloads of answers to scientific questions pointed to the possibilities. On his deathbed, he spoke of wanting to work with the scientists on the other side and come back with newly acquired knowledge. I think Dad would have been very intrigued with the concept of otherworldly beings promoting scientific advancements in the physical realm.

After my father passed, I knew there was one item of his that I wanted… his clipboard. It was the one item he touched more than all other things combined. The projects it held demanded his attention, challenged him, fed his ego, and connected him with Spirit. In some ways, it signified the "fifth child" in our home, the one that received all of our father's attention.

I see some of my father in me. During the past five years, my attention has been addictively consumed with wanting to understand the ways of Spirit. Rather than a clipboard, pencil, and graph paper, I hold a laptop. Like my father, I am sure to the average observer, it looks like I am daydreaming or wordsmithing my work. In reality, I am in the zone of meditation, connecting with my spirit guides, being fed, being challenged, and feeling fulfilled.

chapter twelve

A Tough Day in Earth School

"Healing doesn't mean the damage never existed.
It just means the damage no longer controls our lives."
-Akshay Dubey

No one ever promised us that life would be easy. We are constantly bombarded with fear and difficulty. Sometimes, we are the ones unknowingly making life harder for someone else.

PAST LIFE FATHER AND SON KARMA

My niece has a male friend, Adam, who has become extremely important to her; they share a close soul connection that many people may not ever experience in their lifetimes. One night, my niece told Adam about my ability to read energy. He requested an intuitive show and tell. He would tell me the name of a friend and I would tell him what his energetic relationship was with that person, in present time. He asked me about his family members and his dog that had recently passed away. Apparently, what I saw was quite accurate as he kept asking about more and more acquaintances. Our conversation was intriguing, and I could sense that this activity led him to a greater understanding of some problematic relationships, which in turn led to some acceptance and healing.

Adam and his father Lance have a complicated and painful relationship. The relationship between father and son was centered on love, yet, there has been a history of a great deal of fighting between them. Adam described his father as frequently angry, hostile, and prone to bullying. Adam, in turn, is protective and guarded, tired of not being accepted, and becoming increasingly combative with his dad. Compounding the problem is that Adam is effeminate and openly gay. Lance has stated that he wishes he could change that about his son. The mother's role has been to serve as a buffer between the two males. She has been on the receiving end of both Adam's and Lance's verbal assaults herself.

In the physical realm, I have met Lance a few times. He was always polite with me, but I sensed very dark lower level energies. Our home has served as a safe place for Adam to come when life at home got too uncomfortable.

The night Adam learned of my intuitive abilities, his father, Lance, showed up unannounced in spirit form for healing. Spirit to spirit communication is very quick and effective. As typical, in the middle of the night, I was woken from my sleep by the sense of a being or soul seeking help.

Here was Lance in my space, politely seeking healing. I immediately saw that he had been significantly wounded emotionally, and perhaps physically, as a young boy. These wounds were so deep that they stopped his emotional development, and he presented to me as an adult-sized soul being commandeered by a young, hurt boy. Angels flocked in for his healing. As the wounds were being healed, I was able to see his spirit age beautifully without being influenced by the trauma of his childhood. I saw him as a young man holding his newborn son, Adam, excitedly loving him and full of expectation for a life well-lived. I watched Dad, in spirit, age into the robust soul of his current age. Lance and Adam's relationship was karmically updated into present time and space without the overlaying toxic hurt of the past.

After the healing, I looked at Lance's relationship with his son. It seemed significantly healthier in its updated version, but I saw that Lance was not feeling loved or accepted by his son. He was feeling judged, and not living up to Adam's expectations left Lance feeling unlovable. I wondered what that was about and looked to see if they had shared a past life that was impacting their relationship in current time.

I saw a past life that they shared, and indeed, it was fraught with drama. But in that lifetime, Adam was the father and Lance was the son. Adam had not only been a hostile and angry father but also mean, dismissive, and abusive. Lance did not live up to his father's expectations, and Adam was quick to point that out. In this current lifetime, Lance carried the cellular memory in his DNA of being judged and facing the disapproval of Adam, now his son.

It is interesting to watch karma play out in relationships. In the past life, the aggressive father traumatized the son. In this life, the victim is now the father seeking retribution for past hurts.

Through the grace of the angels and akashic record keepers, healing was provided to the past life, karmic rings closed, and Lance and Adam's relationships updated into current time.

I also saw that the mother's relationships with her husband and son were updated into current time to allow for growth and change. After all the updating and healing, it was now time for a collective exhale and a group hug!

The life lesson I learned from Adam and Lance was that whatever I dish out to someone will karmically come back to me.

Doctor, Heal Thyself

I had a hard time a few months back. I felt like the radio show the night before had gone okay, but then the feedback from my producer was that I would have more listeners if I was more conversational and read less. She suggested I have a co-host, which felt like a failure to me. I wanted the purity of my message; I didn't want to be distracted, and I was doing exactly what Spirit was guiding me to do. I told her thank you, but no thank you. I had a lot of content to share and wanted to get through it. But to be honest, it hurt. Maybe my self-talk was right: I wasn't smart enough. I wasn't good enough. My best was none too good.

Everything that happened for the rest of the day compounded that feeling. I sought validation from emails and Facebook posts, neither of which ever came. Once again, I was in a place of seeking and needing validation. Hadn't I already been through this? But this time I had one more layer that I could add to it. Now I could add that no one was interested in my radio show. Never mind the fact that I had only recorded three shows.

Maybe I didn't have a message that was worth listening to. Perhaps the problem was not the message, but the messenger. I called my friend Denice who is my number one supporter. She reinforced the things I needed to hear: that I did make a difference in the world and that my message was an important one. Maybe I had just not found the right audience. She reminded me that I had helped people in my private sessions using intuition and my connections to the archangels and Divine Mother.

Denice assured me that my time spent as a writer was not wasted. She reminded me that I have an audience in the ethereal realm and that it's harder to assess their validation. We also talked about how in the ethereal realm, the audience will change based on what they need to hear. Maybe that happens in the physical realm as well, that the audience will vary based on the need.

Still, a pervasive sense of, "You are wasting your time" was weighing heavily on me over the weekend. I woke in the middle of the night, and I saw myself as a spiritual being. I was being embraced by Divine Mother. I saw her reach into my eye and pull out a huge worm-like being that didn't belong to me. I immediately felt my doubts about my purpose and my abilities release. I saw that I had picked up foreign energy and had allowed it to permeate my thoughts, beliefs, and actions. Thank you, Denice, for the reality check, and Divine Mother for the healing.

It'll All Come out in the Wash

I thought about sitting down to write, but I was feeling fatigued. Instead, I sat outside and went into meditation. I stopped to listen to my body, and I felt jittery exhaustion as if my nervous system was running poorly on adrenalin. I know when my body feels anxious, angry, or sad that an old story or belief is preparing to break loose so a new truth can emerge, which will push me to grow.

I sat with my emotions and listened to my body. I saw a vision of myself in spirit wearing a t-shirt with writing on it. That wouldn't come as a surprise to my friends, as many of the clothes in my closet are emblazoned with words, or names of places I have visited. I looked down and read across my chest: **"Stay small! Don't put yourself out there."** I don't remember paying money for that one, but my guess is I have paid a hefty personal price for believing it. Archangel Michael asked me to give him the shirt. I handed it to him. He dumped it in a vat of liquid in front of him, and the shirt came out blank; all the writing had been removed. How easily the words evaporated, as if they were never real. Interestingly, I was not feeling as jittery as I had been before.

I looked down and saw I was wearing a different t-shirt. It read, **"Why bother? No one will read it."** I knew this was in reference to the book that I was creating. Archangel Michael said, *"Give me that shirt,"* so I did. Again, he dunked it in the liquid, and the shirt came out blank. I understood that the words on that shirt were my old story that I had used to keep myself small. The words no longer existed, were no longer valid, and had no hold on me. I checked in with my body, and the jitters were completely quieted.

I looked down again at the new t-shirt I was wearing. It read, **"I'm not that good of a writer."** Not a very catchy slogan, but I liked it enough to let it stop me from striving to become a syndicated newspaper columnist. I handed it to Archangel Michael and watched as the shirt went into the vat of liquid. Yep, it came out blank.

One last time, I looked at the new shirt I was wearing, and it read, **"No one wants to hear my message."**

I looked at Archangel Michael and said, *"Please."* He took the shirt from me, dunked it in the liquid and the words disappeared.

As Archangel Michael removed all of the old messages, I realized that they were just words that I chose to keep figuratively, and in this case literally, close to my chest. No one made me wear the t-shirts; I held onto those beliefs with my own free will. I checked in with my body, and my fatigue had disappeared.

With four layers of damning, stinkin' thinkin' self-talk removed, my t-shirt was a blank slate. Nothing was keeping me from creating my new truth. If I had the ability to create the messages that impact my heart and actions, why not choose words that support myself? And support my work? My new T-shirt reads, **"I am worthy, my messages are valuable, and souls will be touched as a result of my sharing what's in my heart."** Thank you, Archangel Michael!

Channeled from the Divine Mother through Sumaya O'Grady,
Excerpts from "Communicating with Divine Mother," Walking
with Spirit Radio Podcast, International Angels Network,
August 9, 2018

Ruth: Is there anything that mother Mary would like to share with us today?

Sumaya: Beloved Mother Mary, do you have a message for the listeners of this beautiful show here with Ruth Anderson?

Yes, Beloved. I would like to tell all of the listeners that the most important thing right now is to really deeply trust that things are going according to the divine plan. That we understand that there is a fair amount of stress and perhaps deep concern about all of the changes that the Earth is going through and the changes on the planet with many painful truths that are now coming to light that people are grappling with. We want everyone to understand that this is all in divine order and that ultimately there will be a greater light that will be manifesting for the planet Earth after everything is said and done. It is a matter of trust and for each person to follow their own heart's guidance about how to be with this. But to know that many, many guides and ascended masters and angels are working very deeply with the people of Earth right now as we go through this very challenging and perhaps very exciting period of awakening, which is much like a birth. And birth may be painful at times. But at the end, you have a beautiful child, something new and something special that's never come forth before. This is what is looked for now with the birth of the new energies here on planet Gaia, and all that's possible for everyone that lives here.

So, it's important to have faith in that, and to always continue to ask for guidance to any of the ascended beings that you feel drawn toward. Toward the Divine Mother, toward God, however you understand that, according to your religion. It does not matter what name you use but continue to tap into your own divine source. And to see that you are a divine being and that you have chosen to be here on the earth for this time… and to have heart about that and to know that you have a role to play. Whatever that is will be revealed to you. Blessed be.

Ruth: Thank you so much and I have to tell you that is exactly the question I was going to ask. I was going to ask if she had any advice for people who were afraid or worried about the direction of the world.

Sumaya: There is a tremendous amount of divine support. She has spoken about this in the past in other situations too. She has spoken about this a lot because people want to know what is going to happen.

chapter thirteen

Affirmations on Healing

One way that Spirit speaks to me is through the act of writing. I might be given the title of a vignette, then when I sit down to write it, the rest of the message flows to me. Or I might be given the ending first, and then the beginning of the story makes itself apparent. The following vignettes were written with Spirit, about times when I was healed or that were composed for the healing of others. As I wrote this, Archangel Michael said that he hoped that the readers would read each vignette and feel a connection to Spirit in their own lives or see where they could be more connected.

VULNERABILITY

I woke up the other morning feeling very vulnerable. What is vulnerability? I decided that it is the gut-wrenching awareness that you are completely alone. If you are truly alone in the world, this means any power has to come from within yourself. This feeling can cause fear, and when you give into that fear, you can become incapacitated. Giving into vulnerability and allowing it to dictate what you do in the morning, is giving in to low level energies. Low level energy wants you to give up and stay small.

How do we get out of low level energy? Call on the Divine, ask them to be with you and to guide you and support you. Bring in divine healing light. Bring it down through your crown and fill your aura.

Please remember that you are not alone. If you are seeking personal power, your sense of self can be fortified and emboldened by having the Spiritual Divinity standing right next to you. Simply open your heart and mind and ask warrior angels to come in and surround you. You are only as vulnerable as you allow yourself to feel.

THE OXYGEN MASK

If you have ever flown on an airplane, you have heard the advisory warning to put your oxygen mask on first before attempting to assist others around you. I was reminded of this advice when I got in the car one morning to take my daughter to school and my mother to the doctor. I noticed two warning lights on my dashboard: the first told me that my car needed fuel and the second, that it was time to change my oil. I was struck by the reminder that although I'm part of the sandwich generation and I'm expected to be present and available for both my children and my parents, I must take care of myself first: physically, emotionally, and spiritually, or I will not be able to assist others in their time of need.

A Lightworker in the Darkness

So, what happens when a lightworker has a bad day? Ever wake up and feel kind of sad? Ever feel anxious due to life circumstances that you have no control over? Sometimes I do. But thankfully, not very often. On the days I feel that way, I wonder what it says about a lightworker who works with clients to help them get out of their own funk, but who is clearly sitting in her own funk. Does that mean I am not an effective intuitive healer? Does that mean that I am just choosing to wallow in self-pity or anxiousness and am choosing not to use the energetic skills that I have? Does it mean that I have done a poor job of keeping the anxious or depressed energy of others from impacting me personally? Maybe.

But, maybe all it means is that I am human. As I have never claimed to be anything but human, I guess that's okay. I am very careful to only work with others when I am sure that I have a solid connection with my guides and God and possess clear knowingness. I will not pretend to be anything other than what I am. And when I am done wallowing, I will clean out the energetic stew I am in and look to the heavens for my inspiration and guidance. And just like that, this lightworker will be back in the light.

Being Human in a Lightworker's Body

Are lightworkers supposed to be immune from experiencing anything other than walking in the light and being an inspiration to others? Are we to assume that they are never angry, never sad, never gloomy? How can a lightworker bring light into the world when sometimes they are surrounded by darkness and they choose to stay that way? Does a lightworker need to be immaculately walking with Divinity, or is it okay to be a human who experiences the emotions of life that are sometimes not happy or full of light? I think most lightworkers that write publicly tend to write only when they are feeling upbeat and capable of presenting a positive front. But do they ever have times that they feel gloomy and less than inspirational? I'm sure they do, but if we only hear from people when they feel great, we get a limited perspective on their true-life experiences. This can lead to self-doubt and judgement among other lightworkers, who are aware of their own human weaknesses. I am here to tell you that 98% of the time this lightworker is positive, uplifting, and capable of leading others with inspiration or divine healing. There are other times when I feel a little overwhelmed with what it feels like to be a human in a body on Earth. I think my task is to accept with grace and humility that I am merely human and that it would be unconscionable to expect of myself any less... or frankly, any more.

Two Steps Forward, One Step Back

I sat at lunch with my good friend Monica Augustine talking about the emotional ups and downs and being a lightworker in a human body. I was feeling particularly unsure of myself, my goals, and ultimately my path. We talked about how sometimes even lightworkers need to take time to assimilate all that they have learned and really absorb new life lessons before they feel ready and prepared to move forward. I told her I felt like I had a big, imaginary question mark over my head and that I was only comfortable feeling like I had exclamation points over my head. When I feel those exclamation marks, I am enthusiastic and confident in myself and where I am going. For me to feel those question marks over my head was very disconcerting and troubling.

Monica said how crucial it was for a lightworker to understand being in a funk, being unsure, or even sad. She said, "How else would you be able to empathize and understand what your clients are going through if you have never felt those thoughts yourself?" She continued, "As for always needing to feel a certain way 100 percent of the time to be able to help others, I think is a myth of perfection. I think we all feel many things in a given day, week, or month. I think it's more about our intention and our dedication to helping and serving. No one expects us to be perfect or feel all the 'perfect' feelings or emotions, as if there were any, except us."

"The Bible says sometimes Jesus was unsure and, 'Why hast thou forsaken me?', right? But he kept doing what he felt was right and his to do. Many people in their field and many experts, have had these questions. I think we just keep trusting, following our inspirations and observing the journey."

We were able to look back together at our individual growth steps on our journeys as healers, and we saw times of growth and times of assimilation followed by times of growth and then times of assimilation. I explained that I had been very resistant to this time of assimilation; we both knew that resisting would only make this time persist. I would not give myself the grace to move and grow if I was resisting the lesson. I was able to see that this downtime has been a growth step. Learning things that I was not comfortable with resulted in feeling like I was stuck and not moving forward. And sometimes, learning an uncomfortable lesson has been as important, if not more important, than having a comfortable peak experience. Thank you, Monica, for your wise counsel.

I also saw that I was overwhelmed by trying to do everything by myself: creating workshops, writing a second book, designing women's retreats, posting on Facebook, my website, and marketing my book while simultaneously raising children, running a household, and helping my ill and aging parents. I can't punish myself for not getting more done every day. I was trying to take on three or four full-time jobs and do them well. It was not humanly possible.

So how should I prioritize competing demands? In meditation, I put each activity in its own individual bubble and energetically looked to see which one rose to the top. And that day, the bubble that rose to the top contained my family.

In the Flow

When I'm working on The Ministry and The Ministry Online, I tend to think if I am not writing or putting information out into the world, that my time is not well-spent. In other words, if I am not doing, then I am not worthy. Sound familiar to anyone?

About two months ago, I saw in meditation that I needed to spend time assimilating lessons I had recently learned and to allow myself time to heal on a soul level. I understood that my ability to have a more significant impact in the world relied on my taking this time for me. I knew it wasn't just important; it was imperative. It felt awkward to "sit idle," not knowing my future direction or focus. Even though I struggled, I learned how to be still, listen, grieve, and accept divine timing. Once I was able to stop resisting the fact that I didn't have clarity and learned to enjoy not knowing, the focus and direction of my future were finally made clear to me.

Recently, I felt my energy shift, and I understood that this period of reflection and assimilation was over. The phrase, "In the flow" came to my mind. I was now back in the flow of creation. Once again, I stepped back into the world as a writer and speaker, but this time with more confidence and more depth of understanding. In hindsight, I realized that as a spiritual being, when I am sharing with others, I am in the flow of outward creative energy. Equally valid and relevant, while I was seemingly idle, I was still in the flow of creative energy. The energy flowed inward; it was purposeful as it melted away layer after layer of existing beliefs and life patterns that no longer served me. Some of those constructs were well entrenched, and it was painful to acknowledge and to release them. While I didn't look like I was working, in reality, I was doing a great deal of hard work.

For those of you who feel that you need to be outwardly doing in order to be worthy, there is equal value in taking time to do the inner work. May you be patient with yourself during times of needed respite and recouping.

ACCEPTANCE AND REFRAMING

I provided a spiritual counseling session for Stan. In his late 60's, he had a complicated medical history including falling from the second story onto the ground doing construction work, followed by two bouts of dysentery during travelling. The last 40+ years of his life had been wrought with fatigue, significant digestion issues, lack of thirst or hunger, and the need to rest 3 or 4 times a day. Over the years he met with many doctors, specialists, and energy healers.

I looked at Stan energetically. I heard Indian music; I saw him in a mass of souls with whom he could commiserate and connect. His energetic body was broken at his lower back, which did not allow for the movement of energy between his upper and lower body.

I watched as my guides came into the room. Divine Mother, Archangel Michael, Archangel Raphael, Archangel Gabriel. Wait, who is this? There was a being I recognized but I didn't know his name. I first saw him in the shape of a statue: a God with an elephant's head. I looked him up online and identified him as Ganesh, the most famous Hindu God. Lord Ganesh is the remover of obstacles and the Lord of beginnings. He is prayed to at the beginning of any undertaking, and whenever a devotee faces insurmountable problems in their life or otherwise "gets stuck"—that's when he can arrive to clear the way. I was pleased and honored to see this Hindu God and was excited to see what our healing session would consist of.

Stan expressed regret that because of his health he had not been able to realize his life's purpose.

I started working with Reiki energy. Using Byoson scanning, I surveyed where he had stuck energy in his body. My attention was drawn to his intestines, his right hip, and the area of his spine where he had his spine fused. As I worked with the Reiki energy on his abdominal area, I felt a gurgling sound moving throughout his intestines. Divine Mother came and held her hand on Stan's left hip. Archangel Michael hovered above. I switched to his right hip. Divine Mother put one hand on each of his hips. Archangel Michael stood at Stan's feet and had one hand on each of the soles of Stan's feet. I stepped back, held space, and felt the healing energy. Then Lord Ganesh laid a thick blanket of healing over Stan. We sat for a few minutes of quiet healing.

I asked Stan what he thought his life purpose was. He thought of his spirituality. I looked back at his energy before coming into this lifetime. His energy out on the threshold showed very bright golden energy, which represents connection to Spirit. I asked him, "Do you have to be healthy to fulfill this life purpose?"

He answered, "No." But the vision he had for how to fulfill his purpose wasn't possible, with his physical condition.

Stan's gift is that he can process and assimilate a great deal of spiritual information and then break it down to teach others in a way they can easily understand.

I saw him teaching others, but he could not travel to teach workshops. I saw that he needed to reframe how he could teach; maybe he could create podcasts out of the comfort of his living room. Then I saw that he needed to reframe who his audience was: the audience could consist of others who were also incapable of traveling to workshops due to their health issues.

I saw him teaching masses of people who were in a situation similar to his.

After settling into the healing modalities, I looked at his chakras and the underlying organs. I saw his abdominal area was black and dead. As I looked behind the black area, I saw a gaping wound. He thought it represented his inner child or inner children crying out in pain.

I asked what percentage of the time he was in resistance to his physical limitations versus how much of the time he was in acceptance, understanding, and appreciation of his situation. He stated that he was in resistance and wanting his situation to change more than 50% of the time. He realized that by being in opposition to what had been his reality for over 40 years, he was creating a war within himself. He was at war with what was real, and he was ultimately the victim of that war.

As I looked at the gaping wound, I saw grief. Grief for what his reality was. I saw that the depth of his grief matched what his listeners would have been going through as well. Who better to teach others in this misery than someone who has been through it himself?

I saw that only when Stan was in this space of acceptance, could he work to help and teach others. To truly help others, he needed to spend more time in an attitude of acceptance of what was and what could be.

I encouraged Stan to stop fighting what was, and when he had those moments of "I hate this," to stop, reframe, and say, "This just is." Then he could try to accept it, find something to learn from it, and discover how to use that lesson to help others. Every time he found himself thinking "poor me" thoughts for the next few days, he would stop and reframe his thoughts.

My time with Stan showed us both a life lesson: that sometimes in order to move forward, you might need to stop fighting what isn't, accept what your reality is, and move on with new definitions of what is possible and how you can achieve it.

In Need of a Boost

At times on this journey, I waited for the Divine to come to me. I wanted them to come remind me that I was on the right track, and that I was to be ministering and doing intuitive work. One such day, I waited, frustrated and empty.

I heard, *"It is not about the intuitive work. Go back to the concept of Open Clinic. It is not about the intuition, but about the Divine bringing healing made accessible to the masses in human form. What are you doing to promote that?"*

I was waiting for someone Divine or in a body to tell me I should. My thought received a swift response.

"Why?!? Do other preachers wait for the person they will be preaching about to ask them to please do it... again and again? No, they have a conviction to get out and preach their truth. Without being asked."

Okay, so what stupid human games can I put aside today and start moving forward to tell my truth?

Are you like me? Are you waiting for someone to come along and tell you to get out there and speak your truth? Well, in case you are, listen up. Get out there and speak your truth! Live your life as only you can live it!

Comfort Food

Where does your comfort come from? When you are seeking a source of support, an ear to listen, or someone to fill that void in your heart, where do you go? Do you look to a friend, a relative, or go shopping, hoping that you can find something in the store that would help fill that void? Do you turn to food, drugs, or alcohol hoping to numb the pain? When all you have left at the end of the day is you and the hole in your psyche, how do you find the strength to keep moving forward?

When my soul searching has resulted in nothing more than my soul being sucked dry, I know that strength just can't come from me alone. My only way out of this funk is for me to go upwards. I find I have no other option but to call out to my angels and my divinity.

I am reminded of the Bible verse, Psalm 121:1-2. **"I will lift up mine eyes unto the hills, from whence cometh my help. My help comes from the Lord, which made heaven and earth."**

I then surround myself with the loving energy of Divine Mother and God. Why did I wait so long to use this source of comfort that is readily available?

Section Four

Love

chapter fourteen

Love Through Community

The first three years of my intuitive journey, I was quite lonely. Sure, I had friends and family. I even had one friend I could share my stories with, but all she could do was listen and ask questions. Denice fed my soul, but not my insatiable need to understand and learn more. My classmates and teacher had their own experiences with intuition, but they didn't have mine. Again, I could share with them, but they couldn't answer my questions or see the things that I had seen. I wanted badly, but couldn't find, that one person on whom I could rely to walk next to me, or better yet, one step in front of me.

LOOKING FOR A MENTOR

I wrote this while in a difficult place of despair and loneliness:

When words fail me and mentors can't be found

I was looking for someone to say, "I get it, I know, I see it too. I know where you are going, for I have been there myself."

But it's quiet. Too quiet.

Looking for someone, anyone, to say this is your path. Look at your progress.

But it's quiet. Too quiet.

How can a mere human mentor me when the places I go are otherworldly?

No, I need to go inward, go upward to hear the voices, see the angels and guides that have brought me thus far, for them to lead me further.

I am in this world, not of this world. My guidance, my path, my future comes from the Divine.

So inward and upward. What is my next step? Where does this path lead? If there were no barriers, what would I be doing?

Search for Community

I waited a long time to find someone who my soul recognized as "home." Don't get me wrong, I have long-time friends whom I adore, but I had an inkling that there were folks who could truly understand me, and that I could have a profound, instant connection with them once we finally found each other. Maybe it took so long because I was looking in the wrong places, or maybe it was so I could find that place of home in myself first. Perhaps, I needed to evolve and change into someone they would recognize and gravitate to when we finally met.

For whatever reason, this past year I have been able to make the acquaintance of several soul sisters with whom I feel such alignment.

Finding My Tribe

- Late 2017, I felt a nudging to go to a Hay House conference for writers. As the event was in another state, I was reticent about going until a friend said he was interested. When we arrived, there were over 100 participants in the hotel banquet room. I sat in the second row thinking that I would learn more if I was up close and making myself pay attention. I made a point to reach out to a couple of women near me. One lovely woman in the seat directly in front of me had a warm, inviting smile. Her name was Linda, and she had followed the nudging she received to make the trip from California. Day two of the conference, my body grew tired of the stiff hotel chairs, so I moved to the wall and sat on the floor. The beautiful soul from the front row took my lead and followed me to the wall. We started up a conversation that over time turned into a soul sister connection. Linda Dierks, fellow lightworker, and author, not only followed me to the wall, but onto my weekly radio podcast, and to write her first book. Had either one of us not listened to the whispers of Spirit, I don't know if we ever would have connected. I am so honored to have found Linda and enjoy her friendship as we walk on our spiritual journeys together.
- Spring, 2017, I received a request to provide a long-distance personal reading session. When I answered the phone, I instinctively knew that I was supposed to know this client better and saw a vision of us working toward a common goal. Dr. Nancy Tarr Hart listened to her spiritual guidance, recognized my name when she saw it, and reached out. Together we share common interests and experiences that make our hearts beat and add meaning to our lives. While Nancy and I have never met in person, my soul recognized her at once.

To all my tribe members, the new and the old, I thank my lucky stars for you daily! Your presence fills me with love, connection, and belonging.

Lightworker 911

One of the benefits of having lightworkers in my tribe is that I have been able to call on them when I needed energetic healing, someone to meditate with, or someone to provide perspective.

After my father passed, my sister and I wanted to give my mother something to look forward to. We offered to take her on a trip to California to see her sister. Traveling with an 87-year-old with dementia, what could go wrong?

Between the airport, flight, luggage pick-up, rental car, and restaurant, Mom had more than a full day before we ever saw her sister. When they were finally united, they sat and chatted for an hour. My aunt wanted to take us all to dinner at their retirement home's restaurant which was nearby. All of the elders headed outside. I assumed we would drive Mom to the restaurant and went to get my car keys. Apparently, my mother had taken off walking without my sister, unsure of the rented walker, and unaware of the steep driveway. When I got to the front door, I saw my mother halfway down the driveway, walker out of control, trying to catch her balance. Time stood still, and everything seemed like it was moving in slow motion. I called out meaningless sounds of warning, as did my cousin. My sister was several feet away and saw Mom just as she spun and toppled onto the concrete, hitting her head, shoulder, and knee. She lay prone on the ground unable to move. We called 911 and mentally prepared for what could be our horrifying new reality.

I went inside to grab Mom's identification cards. In the bedroom, I stopped to enlist the help of my guides. I immediately felt Divine

Mother out on the driveway with my mother. In the car on the way to the hospital, I felt Archangels Michael and Raphael supporting me, and Divine Mother with Mom in the ambulance. Truth be told, I have a visceral reaction to hospitals; I appreciated that two archangels were bolstering me! I texted my lightworker friend Linda who provided a loving distance healing for Mom. The staff at Loma Linda Hospital Emergency Room wheeled her into triage immediately. From the ER, I reached out to the radio hosts of International Angels Network, and they surrounded my mother with a circle of loving prayer. Within three hours Mom was released from the hospital with no broken bones. The loving support of my light working friends and the Spiritual Divinity was priceless.

Blessings in the Desert

My family went to Santa Fe for a long weekend. Busy with family time, I didn't take much time for meditation. On our last morning there I kept feeling an urging to go inward and meditate, as if some lesson or learning was waiting for me. Getting packed and out of the house, I didn't get to turn inward until we were on the airplane heading home. As I sat in meditation at 33,000 feet, I saw me standing in the desert with my guides, but also with some other women I didn't recognize. My robe was off-white with a tinge of gray, it felt earthy yet goddess-like, flowing, yet simple. The energies of the desert felt different than any I had experienced before. The frequencies were about 6 inches high from the dry desert floor, taller and not as frenetic as wood nymphs; shorter and not as lively as water nymphs. Looking down on the view, the guides were off to one side, and I was on the outside edge of a round space.

It felt like some kind of a ceremony, like an attunement of sorts. I was handed a weathered stick that was my height, and it had a wiggling snake on the top. I held it like a scepter. It was a symbol of me being at one with the earth and being a goddess of the earth. Everything felt Shamanic in nature.

I noticed two other females with me. I recognized them as Linda Dierks and Nancy Tarr Hart. Each of us was ourselves in spirit form, each younger than our physical selves, yet I knew exactly who they were. They were standing on equidistant locations in the circle, creating a triangle with me. Linda and Nancy's robes were similarly colored. All three of our gowns were slightly different styles, all simple, flowing, and goddess-like. Linda wore a ring of flowers around her head like a flower child of the 60's. Nancy was holding a weathered book.

I saw that Linda, Nancy, and I each had our separate connection to the earth, our own gifts, own methods and work, each slightly different from each other. But we were all somehow very much aligned in purpose and with guides in common. We were all three equals in strength and power. Separate, but unified.

The guides continued to stay on the outside of the circle to one side, yet they were participating and not just observing. The feeling I got was that we three were being presented/acknowledged in the ethereal realm. We received blessings for our continued work. The ceremony was loving, reverent, and felt like we were given added power and reach as lightworkers as a result.

Afterward, Nancy explained to me that the serpent is the symbol of wisdom. Awesome!

Come Dance with Me

In meditation, I was with just a few of my guides: Divine Mother, Archangels Michael, Gabriel, and a female archangel I didn't recognize. I am always intrigued to see who is and isn't in attendance. I asked the new angel some questions.

Do other people know you by name?
No.
Can I know you by name?
Yes.
Do you have to do with stamina?
No.
Do you have to do with fortitude?
Yes.
Are you here to help me have more fortitude?
No.

I was taken back to the place of my Reiki attunement. Everything looked familiar. I saw flowers in the valley, and I was reminded how I danced with others.

Were you there?
Yes.

I saw a memory of me dancing with her.

You belong with us.

I felt an intense sense of community.

Were there other archangels there?
Yes.

I felt such joy and connection.

Was it the Reiki attunement that got me there?
Yes.

Do you have to do with Reiki energy?
No.

Does the Reiki energy open people to the world of the archangels?
Yes. Come back to this place when you forget who you are, or when you are tired and need to remember.

Thank you
Come dance with me.

I sensed my friend Linda Dierks.

Is Linda here?

Yes.

Is Nancy Tarr Hart here?

Yes.

I thought so because I could feel them. Were they there at my first Reiki attunement?

Yes.

Are they my soul sisters?

Yes.

Divine Mother, is there anything else?

I love you.

I love you, too.

I spoke to the female archangel.

I didn't ask you your name.

I heard something that sounded like Athena.

Athena? Is your name Athena?

Yes/no.

I thought maybe I was close, but wasn't sure.

I looked up Athena on the internet. Here is what I read: "Roman equivalent: Minerva. Athena, also referred to as Athene, is a very important goddess of many things. She is goddess of wisdom, courage, inspiration, civilization, law and justice, strategic warfare, mathematics, strength, strategy, the arts, crafts, and skill." (https://greekgodsandgoddesses.net/goddesses/athena/)

Do you want me to call you Athene?

No.

Do you want me to call you Athena?

No.

Do you want me to call you Minerva?

Yes.

Are you the same Minerva that came to me in California and Washington State?

Yes.

Coming Home

In meditation, I saw myself walking along a stream, fishing. I was with a male archangel.

I wondered which archangel this was.

Archangel Michael?

No.

I didn't think so.

Archangel Raphael?

Yes.

Nice! It feels like I haven't seen you for some time!

Together we walked up the stream. I recognized a spirit nearby as Nancy.

Is Linda here?

Yes.

I fell to my knees crying.

I am so fatigued! I have been working so hard!

Linda sat with me on the ground, and we played, pulling out the yellow bits of a dandelion. I laughed; being with her was so sweet. Then she said, "Come on, dance with me!" I stood up and the three of us laughed and danced to music only we could hear.

Archangel Raphael, I missed you.

I was here all along.

I saw Jesus walk over toward me. I went to him and fell to my knees; He gave me a blessing to do my work.

Thank you!

chapter fifteen

Palpable Love

In conversation with Divine Mother during meditation:

Love is a thing. Love is a thing that you give to someone else.

How about giving it to yourself first?

Yes, if you don't love yourself, it is hard to be able to love someone else.

Are the many faces of Divine Mother the many faces of love?

Yes.

I sensed that my time with her was over.

Is there anything else?

Yes.

A huge ball of energy, love, came from Divine Mother to and throughout me. It resonated in my heart space and body. The feeling was full, robust, packed with nurturing rich energy.

That is what love feels like! For the first time, I understood that real love was something I could see and feel, and I was changed as a result of having experienced it. What I have been putting out to others has been a much watered-down version of that. I will concentrate on that and have intentions of sharing a more profound, richer love.

LOVE IN ACTION

My sister and I found ourselves on an unexpected road trip across the heartland of America. She is an avid quilter, and her friends told her about the wonders of the Missouri Star Quilting Company, a mecca for quilters consisting of thirteen specialty stores in Hamilton, MO. While the stores were 90 minutes off of our path, we made the side trip to Hamilton. My sister was like a child on Halloween! It was great fun watching her excitement. It was so easy for me to drive out of our way and give her some uninterrupted time to shop. As I drove across town to find a spot for lunch, I heard the words, *"Palpable love."* How easy it can be to give someone a gift of palpable love, leaving them feeling loved, really loved.

MI AND GOD

I sat in meditation and went to join God. Very quickly, God removed all cellular aspects of my body; I was reduced to vapor. My eye was drawn to a small black metal-looking box that was left where my body had been just moments before. God set fire to the box. As it burned, I wondered if this was the last aspect of my connection to otherworldly beings. The box turned silver before being burned beyond recognition. Then it was blown aside.

I showed back up in the form of Mi, my higher self. She faced God and curtsied as a sign of fond, familiar reverence. She sat at God's feet, looking comfortable as if she has spent a great deal of time there previously.

I saw that Mi had angelic wings. I knew that she wore them at times. Mi was sitting contently talking. She wasn't asking for anything, reciting anything ritualistic, but merely chatting and enjoying God as if she was speaking with a close friend. It felt like God was enjoying her presence in turn.

I realized, in retrospect, how little quality time I, in body, spend with God. My time with God is right at the beginning of my meditation time. Honestly, I sit at God's feet with the hope of receiving something, albeit energetic healing or something that will change my perspective or give me guidance on next steps. I don't know if I have ever just sat, chatted, and not had the goal of walking away transformed. Yet Mi had spent time doing just that. And she benefited from enjoying another aspect of God that I am not familiar with.

Leaving God's side, I had several questions. I turned to Archangel Michael.

Does God see us in the form of our highest self all of the time?

No.

Does God see us as our physical bodies with all of the trappings of the world?

No.

Or does God see us only as a soul?

No.

How does God see us?

God is not a man. God doesn't view you as this or that. He just holds you in love. He does not need words to define the love with which he has for you.

Do you think of God as a he?

No, but you do. That's why I refer to God that way.

Language of the Heart

I went to God in meditation and immediately dissolved except for my heart. I was observing from about a foot away. I saw my heart being held in loving hands; I assume God's. I watched my heart beat and felt somewhat detached and at the same time wholly connected to my heart.

You... this is all you are, your heart. Without it, you are nothing, not even dirt on the ground.

I wasn't sure if God was referring to my physical heart or the figurative heart that feels emotions. I heard the phrase, "I love you with all my heart." It was not God saying that to me, but just making me aware of the phrase.

The heart is seen as one, both the body organ that pumps blood and the symbolic heart that feels emotions.

I was curious that they are referred to as the same name, for without the one that beats, there is no opportunity to feel. I saw my heart smashed between the two hands, blood dripping, the fibrous tissue condensed to a flat pulp. Surprisingly, I was not horrified or frightened by the scene.

This is what man cares for the heart. Nothing. Wars, murders, man does not care if the heart is silenced and decimated.

Then I saw that my heart was back in its original form, beating steadily and full of life.

My heart became coated in a layer of golden colored protective coating, and the shape became nondescript.

This is how I view each heart.

I saw that it was protected, cherished, revered.

When you give your heart to someone, make sure that they are worthy of receiving it and will protect it, both physically and with their emotions. Likewise, when someone else gives you their heart, be ever so careful to treat it with the respect it deserves.

That which makes your heart beat is love.

Figuratively or literally?

Figuratively.

That which your heart longs for is love.

Your heart and your soul are inextricably intertwined; together they comprise the core of you. The male and female energy that they each are comprised of combine beautifully to encapsulate the core of you. When one is wicked or loves evil, it is the heart that has embraced the darkness. The soul is the runner, transport, or the messenger of the heart's corrupt nature. The heart... I look into the hearts of men. The soul is merely a reflection of the heart. Study the heart; everything you would need to know about a person you will find in the heart.

What about my heart? What does it say about me?

I wanted to stay contemplating my heart.

You can look at it and consider its weight anytime.

I didn't want to go, but my time there was complete.

Come back any time, I have much more to share.

LOVE PERSONIFIED

I sat with God in meditation.

I know you are trying to write this book but don't forget to live in the meantime.

I was immediately reduced to vapor. This time there was nothing left of me but ethers. I noticed smaller vapors near me in varying sizes, each as a diffuse puffball. I recognized their energy as animals I had loved and lost. Then I saw larger vapors and knew them as people I had loved and lost to death.

This love you hold for them is constant. Love never dies.

Is this about love being a thing?

Yes.

Once love is created, it continues to exist? Is that in energetic form?

No.

Is it a real thing?

Yes.

Is it like a see-through string attached to us?

No.

Is it an energy?

No.

Does it have a shape?

Yes/no.

God, can you see it?

No.

God, can you feel it?

Yes.

I couldn't imagine love ethers were stored in a huge cosmic jar somewhere. What good would that do anyone? Maybe the residual love helped the earth in some way.

Does the residual love help the planet in any way?

No.

I didn't think so. Is the residual love attached to the person who did the loving?

Yes.

Is the residual love attached to the person who received the loving?

No.

God, can you feel how much a person has loved others in their lifetime?

No.

Can you see how much a person has loved others in their lifetime?

Yes.

When you see the person and the love that they have felt in their lifetime, does it look like a ring or hula hoop around them?

I thought maybe there was one thin ring for each person or animal that they had loved.

No.

Maybe we become thicker in spirit the more we love.

Is it layers on top of that person's spirit?

No.

Is it how opaque that person's spirit is?

Yes.

If you have loved more, is your spirit more diffused or see through?

Yes.

If you have barely loved at all, is your spirit very opaque?

Yes.

Is that because the more we let others in, the less permeable our protections are?

Yes. Man is here on Earth to love others.

I saw a vision of the Divine Mother as a model for how to love others.

I was shown some of the facets of Divine Mother to think about how to love.

Mother Earth, the abundant gift of nature, trees, and plants, water, and beauty.

Mother Earth is love personified and provides food and sustains life.

Mother Nature is love as well, providing weather, animals, the life force.

Life force? Does Mother Nature provide life to all things on Earth?

Yes.

Without Mother Nature, would there be life on Earth?

No.

So, Mother Earth and Mother Nature are two different things?

Yes.

Do you see them as female?

No.

Do you see them as male?

No.

Did people come up with those names?

Yes/no.

Did you give people those names?

Yes.

Did you choose "Mother" because of the thoughts of love and all that it implies?

Yes.

Are we to look to Mother Earth and Mother Nature for how to love others?

Yes.

Were they gifts of your love?

Yes.

True Joy

Pure joy for me comes when I am in connection to Spirit. That doesn't mean that I can't find joy in situations and people here on earth. It means that if I am not in concert with my higher self, Spirit, and God that I am not free or open to experiencing the joys in the physical realm, because I am weighed down by my old stories and the burdens of the external world.

Section Five

Connection

chapter sixteen

Connection to Self

My time of walking and living with Spirit has enabled me to receive answers to questions about myself that I didn't realize I
had. The Holy Spirit and Archangel Michael prepared my heart by
showing me a few past lives where I was in relationship with souls I
am currently in relationship with. Some of these past life stories ended
badly, in some cases horrifically. I saw how the stories from our past
lives have played out similar emotional chaos into our current lifetime.
The message to me was that sometimes it is difficult to make sense of
our current day relationships. In order to understand them fully, we
might need to explore our past lives in order to seek the healing and
transformation that would help us to heal as souls in bodies now.

I met Denice in 2005 when our daughters were three years old and
in the same preschool program. We became friends mostly because
of the shared experiences that we wanted for our daughters. We were
both somewhat older, vigilant moms who wanted to provide many

learning opportunities for our girls. So, we created opportunities to all experience together. As a result, Denice and I became close even though as they got older, our girls drifted away from each other and made new friends. They still hold a common closeness for shared experiences together growing up, but the real connection at this point was between Denice and me.

A few years back, Denice went through a very difficult divorce, and I tried to be there for her as she was struggling. My husband and I were able to help her locate a house in a safe neighborhood, and Denice and Marie moved in shortly thereafter. Somehow, I felt a strong compulsion to help and protect her.

Denice and I continued to be friends, and we continued to support each other as we walked on our individual paths through this lifetime. Part of Denice's transition during and after the divorce was beginning to pay attention to herself as a whole human being again. She had stopped paying attention to her body during the marriage between full-time work, raising her daughter, and running a household.

One spring day, in the midst of the divorce trauma, Denice was walking her dog at a nearby dog park. She saw a young gentleman with a sign in his car window advertising his services as a personal trainer at a new gym across town. His name was Joe. They got to chatting, and something clicked between them. He invited her to come to work out at his place of business. Joe was young, charismatic, and she was immediately drawn to him.

Over the next several months, Denice worked out religiously at Joe's gym. He showed devotion to her as a client and friend and encouraged her as she sculpted her body and worked through the emotions of the divorce. Denice, in turn, showed a great deal of support for Joe as he grew his business. It was clear to me from the beginning that they had been put in each other's lives for a reason. It was not a coincidence that he happened to bump into her by the dog park that sunny afternoon.

As an enterprising businessman, Joe developed a business model which included sending out homework and inspiration to his clients via technology. Denice gravitated to that level of motivation and attention. It was not long before Denice became a follower of Joe's and I sensed guru energy developing. I was happy for her but uncomfortable with her uncompromising devotion to him that felt beyond rational to me. I kept watching her put Joe on a pedestal, and I was increasingly uncomfortable. I could not make myself meet him, because I knew I could not and would not embrace the guru energy; I could not respect watching her do it, nor could I respect him for allowing it (assuming he was aware of her devotion). My reaction to this scenario was visceral, and I could not explain why I felt so deeply uncomfortable. Was it jealousy that my friend was now looking great physically and had someone who fed her need for attention and inspiration? No, Denice and I had not been that close that I would feel jealous of someone else's participation in her life, and frankly, I was happy that she had an outlet that was life-affirming during this challenging period in her life. My reaction was not one of jealousy, but wary concern for Denice and disappointment and disapproval in Joe for allowing (and maybe fostering) a guru relationship with her, and perhaps other clients as well. Why did I care about his dealings with other clients? I had no idea, but I just knew that I would not be witnessing it myself.

Several times over the years, Denice tried to convince me to meet Joe and sign up to exercise at his gym and have him become my personal trainer. I resolutely held my stance that I was not interested. No matter how many wonderful things she said about him, it wasn't going to happen.

A few years passed. Denice's passion for physical improvement waned, but she was still extremely devoted to Joe. During that time, Joe had been working and learning diligently; he broadened his role from being an exercise expert to also become an energetic spiritual warrior. He had evolved into an inspirational guru as well as a fitness expert, so now his clients were receiving spiritual motivation along with tips about physical fitness. How perfect really; one-stop shopping for creating the complete package of an ideal body and soul! I would hear from time to time how Joe's clients were gravitating to this new level of body/spirit enlightenment. Joe's following was growing, and I sensed the guru energy expanding.

During this same time period, I had been working on my spiritual and energetic journey of recreating myself as an intuitive, so my growth and Joe's were happening at the same time. Denice was surrounded by Joe's influence of inspiration as well as the influence of all my musings about energy and intuition. Joe and I both happened to write books at the same time, and Denice was in the middle of both of them. She was my sounding board when I had questions and needed to discuss concepts with someone. Denice walked beside me as I created my book and dealt with covers, layout, and editing. She walked beside Joe as he created his book. She was the interface between him and his publisher and offered advice about layout and design. We published our books at virtually the same time.

The commonalities of our two journeys were astounding. Denice and I laughed at the timing and similarities and how she was caught in the middle and had no choice but to embrace it all. She was moving forward on her own journey and was flanked by me sharing stories of intuition, angels, and healing, and Joe with his inspirational teachings. Denice didn't stand a chance of escaping her own personal evolution.

During this same time, I was being shown images of Joe and me traveling together and running classes while Denice sat outside our classrooms selling both of our books. I saw visions of myself knowing and working alongside Joe. For this to happen, I knew that there would need to be a shift of the energy as I sensed it, and I understood that it would need to be imminent. I gave Denice a copy of my book to give to Joe. Still, I had not met him. I had resistance to meeting him; I did not have words for it, but I felt it.

A month or so later, Denice requested that I do a Reiki energy healing on her and I gladly helped her out. Then she asked if I would provide healing for Joe. I explained that I would need his permission and that I would do it remotely as I was still not ready to meet him. I knew in my heart of hearts that if I met him in person, I would feel judgment toward some aspect of him, which would crush Denice. Unable to tell Denice no, I said I would try to help him out if he was interested. The minute that I texted that I would provide healing for him, his energy popped forcefully into the room and into my space. I needed to create my own personal barrier around his energy because it was so strong and without boundaries.

A day later I sat to provide the distance healing for Joe. I felt a little uneasy as if I was energetically jittery. I knew I was being energetically triggered and it felt like my intuitive skills were on display as well as on trial. Knowing how important Joe was to Denice, I really wanted the reading to be beneficial for him, although the outcome, of course, was out of my hands. Thankfully, I had no problem connecting with Spirit and seeing his healing commence. When I connected with Joe's spirit at the time of the reading, it felt quite familiar. I was curious about that as we had still never met, but I let that go. During the reading, I put all that I had seen and experienced into writing and sent it to him. Joe was quite struck with the information that I shared. He immediately wrote back with many questions, and I tried to answer them as well as I could, without putting myself back into the intuitive space. With his level of knowledge and spiritual evolution, I was not surprised by his many questions. I felt grateful and validated that he resonated with the information that I shared with him. It was apparent, however, that any future reading with him would be more effective if it took place in person so I could address his questions in current time and not after-the-fact.

Even after sharing the shared energetic connection of the reading with him, I still had a nagging energetic reaction towards Joe. What was all this about?

Joe requested a second session with me. I knew that this next session would need to be in person and that it was finally time for us to meet. We put a date on the calendar. He mentioned wanting to meet with me on a monthly basis. I got a flash of the guru energy, but for a split second, it felt like Joe was putting *me* on a pedestal. That thought made sense to me; as someone who accepts guru energy, he would probably be open to seeing someone else as a guru. I said no. I knew I would not allow myself to become someone's guru. If we were to continue to work together, we would set up one session at a time, as long as it was productive for both of us. My relationship with Joe would not be defined by either one of us being put on a pedestal. Absolutely not.

The next morning during meditation, I walked into Open Clinic. I saw that a celebration was taking place. I looked further to see what was going on, and I saw that Joe, in spirit, was in the center of the celebration. His seemed to be comfortable there, unfazed by the attention; there was no sign of ego or affect. I was very surprised! I had been given celebrations and even parades before but never had I seen a celebration for someone else at Open Clinic. I asked why they were celebrating Joe. I was told that they were celebrating the lessons Joe was about to learn, starting with his reading with me. I was also told that they were celebrating the opening of my intuitive healing business and the fact that Joe would be my first paying client. I wondered how my guides knew Joe so well. Had they already been working with him, or more intriguing, had *I* already been working with him in conjunction with the guides? Were Joe and I simply playing out in the physical realm what had been discussed and decided in the spiritual realm? I was amused and intrigued by all that I had seen.

Soon after that, in a scheduling text, Joe referred to me as "Ruth baby." I immediately felt angry and insulted because I felt disrespected; I felt like I was expected to be one of his groupies. His only contact with me was when I had shown him the purest divinity of Divine Mother and the ancient healing power of Reiki, two entities that I have the utmost respect for. How could he then so cavalierly refer to me as Ruth baby? I spoke with Denice about it, and she said, "That is just Joe!" My thought was, "Well, that's not me. And I hope he sees that when we meet." My reaction was strong and surprising to me. I expected more of Joe, and somehow, he disappointed me. In hindsight, I think my emotional response was so intense because I had seen Joe in his purest form in spirit at Open Clinic, without his ego or the flaws he had in the earthly realm, and that was the Joe I wanted to communicate with.

I set a date for our second session a few days later. I sensed that Joe was beyond eager to have whatever information I could offer him. During the few days before our meeting, several times during meditation or upon waking, I heard myself, in spirit, having a full-blown conversation with Joe. A few times I would say, "Stop, I am not having this conversation now! I will speak with you when we meet." Literally, a few minutes later, I would hear us in continued conversation as if no break in the conversation had happened. It was as if a family member was in the room and conversation flowed freely. It wouldn't make sense to say, "Stop, you are in my space, let's talk on Saturday at 10:00." I have not been that energetically connected with anyone else, that I'm aware of.

Soon it was the morning of Joe's first in-person session. I meditated and walked into Open Clinic. As I walked in, I saw Denice and Joe in spirit walking out. I understood that they had just attended some business meeting with Divine Mother and Reiki. I do not know if my higher self, Mi, was in attendance or not, yet it didn't feel like my presence was unwelcome. I was curious why Denice and Joe were there and why they looked so comfortable there, as if checking in at Open Clinic was common for them. I felt a little competitive and shocked. I thought that I was the only one who had been at Open Clinic, yet here these two were. But wait, why was I jealous that they had been there? Didn't I want someone else, anyone else, to have this experience so I could speak with another human about it? Wasn't I afraid I could never figure out how to take someone else to Open Clinic with me? Shouldn't I be happy that I don't have to figure it out, that other folks can go on their own volition? Yes, absolutely! But I still wondered how it was that these two, who I will be teaching, were meeting with my healing guides? And hey, Denice was the first spirit in a living body to attend Open Clinic. Now I was wondering how that had happened. What really happens in the spiritual realm and how does it impact life here in the physical realm?

A little later that morning, I was meditating and thinking about the people I would be meeting with that day. I thought about a practice I have when I start an intuitive session; I ask the client to say his full name three times. As I thought that, Joe's energy was immediately in my space and I heard him excitedly yelling his name at me three times. I chuckled. My scheduled appointment with him was not to start for nine hours, yet here he was in spirit. The thought came to my mind, "I cannot tell you how excited you are to see me!" I created my energetic boundaries and prepared to meet with Joe later that afternoon.

The day progressed, and it was almost time to leave my house to meet Joe for his reading. I started feeling energetically jittery and nervous. I realized my nerves were based on the high expectations that Joe was putting on our reading from across town. I sensed that he was hoping for and expecting an earthshaking reading. I did not know if I could live up to his expectations. Then I was given the message that there was work or healing in Joe that needed to take place before he could receive that life-altering message.

Both Reiki and Divine Mother were prepared for our meeting, and they showed me that they arrived at our meeting place 10 minutes before I even left my house for the short drive over. There was huge expectation and intensity surrounding this upcoming conversation with Joe. I grounded myself once again and started to drive over to our meeting place. As I drove, I was hearing the conversation that was taking place between Divine Mother, Reiki, Joe's spirit, and my spirit in preparation for the meeting. Ten minutes of discussion took place while I was on my way in the car. When I spoke to Joe in Spirit, I sounded like someone who was close to him and was almost reprimanding him; I was adamantly trying to get a message through to him, and absolutely knowing in my heart of hearts that he could understand what I was saying, but he chose not to fully hear the message. I felt that the upcoming time spent together would be a continuation of this conversation rather than a first-time meeting.

I stepped out of the car at our designated meeting place and was surprised to see Joe in body, as I had never met him before. I had no idea really, what to expect physically but I felt like I already knew him quite well on an energetic level. When I walked in the door, I sensed that he wanted to hug me and I gave him my hand to shake instead, not out of standoffishness, but I needed my interaction with him to be on a spirit to spirit level and not a comfortable, familiar, physical level. Our session was intense, fascinating for me, and I sensed, impactful for Joe. The level of connection between us was oddly confusing. I found myself thinking things like, "I know you know this, Joe!"

In sessions with other clients, the information I share is often about stuck energy, past lives, or relationships. Joe's session was decidedly different. Joe was being instructed; instructed as if he was being reminded of something that he used to know in a past lifetime and needed to be reminded of in this lifetime. The level of instruction coming directly from Reiki and Divine Mother was heartfelt, pointed, and intense. Their expectations of him in this lifetime are huge, and oddly, I felt the same way. Our session together was quite extraordinary. At the end of the meeting, I was still energetically jittery. I knew that there was a past-life connection with Joe that I needed to understand.

Past Life Connections

The next day Denice texted me and asked, "Did Joe kill you in a past lifetime?" I had a visceral, jittery response when I read her message. I did not know if Joe and I shared a common lifetime in the past, but I knew it certainly felt like we had. I meditated and waited for insight. I was given the image of me as his older sister in a past lifetime. I saw that I was responsible for ensuring that he and I were both extremely spiritual, religious, and of pure hearts and character. We answered directly to God, and both had an otherworldly essence that was different from others around us. Our parents were loving, yet diminished in our lives, as our devotion to God was paramount. As the older sister, I had been in the role of advisor, mentor, and at times disciplinarian.

I asked how that shared lifetime was impacting me in this lifetime, in particular in my dealings with Joe. I saw that I understood the level at which Joe's soul had embraced God and spirituality in his past lifetime, and in this lifetime I expected that as his baseline, with any learnings from this lifetime added on top of that. As his sister/mentor/disciplinarian, I felt that he had been caught in the shadow side when he wanted to be a guru figure to his clients, and when he allowed his ego to interfere with being a direct conduit between the Divinity and humanity.

I realized that I was not supposed to meet Joe in person prior to that moment in time. If I saw him behaving in ways that I didn't think were of the light or not in his best interest as a spiritual being, my sisterly judgment of those behaviors would have destroyed my ability to work with him in the future, and neither of us would have understood why. I had not evolved enough in my understanding of myself or of past lives and their potential impact. Because I had needed to clear my energy, I was not ready to meet Joe one minute before I did. With this realization, energy within my being shifted, and my jittery energetic responses to him turned to calm understanding and appreciation.

I was finally able to connect with Joe without fear of my unfair judgment and perceptions, so I cleared and updated my karmic relationship with him into current time. I am looking forward to creating the connection that we are supposed to have in this lifetime, without the overlay of the past.

THANAEL

Wanting to understand more about my strong connection to Joe and my need to protect Denice, I read her energy to see if she and I shared a past life.

In the same lifetime that I was related to Joe, Denice was living in our community and shared our otherworldly, God-intense connection. We were part of a Godly family on earth to help bring people to a higher level of consciousness. That made sense to me. Denice may not have had a lot of experiences being in a body, but that did not mean that she was a new spirit in connection to God and the spiritual realm. Her lack of experience in a body helped me understand why I felt the need to watch out for her in this lifetime. This also explained my visceral reaction to Denice treating Joe like a guru. I knew that in our past life, guru energy was not of God, but of the shadow side of man. Denice was putting man, or to be more specific, Joe, before her God.

I saw that some of the people I should be working with in this lifetime are from the original group from our shared past life, that I called a God family. That might be part of why I didn't want to teach others how to do basic energy healing techniques because my work was to be on a deeper level.

It also explained why Denice was smack dab in the middle of both Joe's and my books. And it explained why he and I were in the same stages of growth. It also made sense why Denice was the first spirit in a living body to show up at Open Clinic. And it made sense why Denice and Joe walked out of a meeting at Open Clinic that felt like a business meeting and were both very comfortable there.

Listening to Joe chant and repeat mantras while I was reading his energy, I could not tell whether he said what he was thinking or if he was merely reciting words. At one point, I heard him say, "Thank you" maybe 12 times in a row. I wondered if he had learned a ritual and thought that that ritual helped him connect with Spirit? I found myself wanting to say "Joe, why are you doing that? Stop doing that because that isn't how you connect with Divinity or purge your energy; that is you doing a ritual instead." That morning in meditation I re-lived that moment during his reading, and I heard myself say, "Why are you doing that, Thanael? Stop it!" I stopped talking when I heard myself say the name Thanael and I wondered if that was his name in the past life where I was his older sister. The name just rolled off my tongue as if I had used it 100 times.

THE GOLD STREAK

I saw some moments from our past life. The setting looked like a Puritan settlement, around the time of the Mayflower. The settlement was very strict about behavior and religion. I was about 16 or 17 years old, and my little brother was approximately 12 years in age. We loved and respected our parents. We did not need to fear them, because our behavior was always very good. Our commitment was to God, and our God was much more than the religion of the Puritan community.

One could look at us and not know that we were different from our community, as our clothing was the same. Our behaviors and morality were the same. We kept our heads covered in deference to God. Our souls were pure. But if one looked at the spirit level, one would see a gold colored streak that showed our lineage to God. We were sent to teach and model how to love God, but not necessarily religion.

Denice was our father's sister. Aunt Rosalynn or Nona as we called her, was older than our father. She was middle-aged and heavy-set. She had brown, shoulder length hair with a slight curl to it. Our aunt had the gold streak, but our parents did not. And she recognized it as soon as we were born. Nona knew it was her responsibility to keep an eye on us to make sure that we kept an open relationship and communication with God while we were living on Earth. Her laugh was large and she found us to be amusing. Nona was widowed at a young age and never had children of her own. Her home was close to ours, and she was a regular at our dinner table.

Nona would have groups of women in her home, and she would speak with them while they sat around the fire. Some of the women would sew and listen while Nona talked about far-reaching ideas of God's love and how God knew each person's soul. This was very different from the strict formalities and fear of God found in the religion of our community. She spoke of a personal relationship with the Divinity. The women did not share their conversations with the men in the community because it would not be tolerated. Such musings would result in both the husband and wife being ostracized by others.

Our parents thought Nona's ideas were strange, but they let me and Thanael go and listen. They understood that we had a close connection with Nona and chose to accept it and keep quiet about it. Nona treated us as if we were her own children. She kept a special close eye on my brother and me. We did not need help learning the ways of the world.

No, we needed someone to help us keep our connection to God alive. She was the constant reminder that we needed.

I served as Thanael's disciplinarian when I thought he was getting out of line. I was stricter on him then our parents were. I held him to the impossible standard of Jesus's behavior and God's impossibly pure heart where no shadow side could enter. I was exacting and demanding to a fault. My aunt Nona would encourage me to lighten up on Thanael when I had been particularly strict in my demands for higher moral action from him. She would laugh at me for my rigid interpretation of God's all-encompassing acceptance, forgiveness, and love. I was not easy for Thanael to live with and not easy for him to live up to. In current day life, I saw that I held the same rigidity regarding a pure moral compass. What I see as teachable moments with my own children may be nothing more than an extreme rigidity of a moral code that only I understand the need to enforce

Seeing this past life with Denice and Joe as family and committed service to a Spiritual God brought clarity and helped me to understand my feelings and behaviors. I was finally able to have a clear understanding of my protectiveness of Denice and my unaltering devotion to God.

chapter seventeen

Connections to My Calling

I understand that part of my purpose for being in this world is to share the message that each of us can connect with archangels, God, and the Divine Mother so they might provide profound love, wisdom, healing, and guidance. I willingly accept and embrace my calling.

Walking with Spirit on a daily basis has provided many loving opportunities for me to receive support, encouragement, and direction. I know without a shadow of a doubt that there are several spiritual beings, more significant, smarter, and better networked than I, pulling strings and lining things up to happen. I have observed Mi in the ethereal realm, meeting with individuals to further my work here on Earth. People, names, and businesses have mysteriously been made known to me and upon my reaching out, opened doors I could not have fathomed possible. While I have not acted on every last suggestion (yet), I have embraced most of them.

Channeled from the Divine Mother through Sumaya O'Grady, Excerpts from "Communicating with Divine Mother," Walking with Spirit Radio Podcast, International Angels Network, August 2, 2018

Sumaya: Beloved Mother Mary, do you have a message for Ruth and myself and for all of the listeners on this beautiful show that is bringing forth spirit so much into the world?

Yes, Sumaya, I wish initially for Ruth to know that there are many blessings coming to her from what she is doing. That she is now engaging in activities that are greatly enhancing and raising the vibrations here on the Earth and that the people on this show are here because their spirits are drawn to what's being shown here and each person is always being guided to the very specific thing that they most need to know. Each person has their own unique and beautiful light to shine. So, it's extremely important that you not compare yourself to others and to see that oh, this person is more talented or has more success, or whatever those thoughts might be. Because those thoughts are really not relevant to who you are as a light, to who you are as a soul.

You must trust your own divine mission, your own sense of who you are and where you're going, and keep opening to that because you can't be anyone else but you. You perhaps can be inspired by other people, but not in the sense of a negative comparison. This is one of the great problems that we see here on the Earth and because so many people are now awakening, this problem is beginning to lessen. However, it is still one of the ways in which the negative energies can come inside and waylay you. So, this is something that we are all here asking you to be on guard against and to really begin to pay attention.

Ask yourself what is my light? What do I have to offer and how can I offer it and know that there are answers? And that they will come. There will always be an answer, even if you don't see it in the moment in which you are asking it. Call on my spirit. Call on the spirit of the Divine Mother however you experience her, and she will answer. Blessed be.

THE RIGHT TOOLS FOR THE JOB

I received an email from someone requesting to do a long-distance private reading with me. I learn something every time I do a reading, so I readily accepted. I had been learning about authentic struggles some people have with low-level energies haunting them. This particular client taught me a valuable lesson about low level energies and my work.

Before we started our session, Sandra insisted that Jesus and Archangel Michael not be in attendance. That should have been my clue to say, "No, I'm sorry, but I can't help." She only wanted her guides, most of whom I did not know. This should have been red flag #2.

I went into the session with good intentions. By not allowing my guides to be present, I was ill-prepared and useless. Anything I suggested, Sandra refuted. I don't know if she was mentally ill, being psychically attacked by low level entities, or perhaps a combination of both. After 40 minutes of listening to her describing a horrific past, sobbing, and screaming at entities she saw in her room, I told Sandra I was unable to help. I felt utterly useless and was not able to combat whatever was making her life miserable.

After that, I struggled with my role as a lightworker. Shouldn't I be able to help everyone? My ego and desire to help others were shaken with not being able to help. I remembered my mentor, Stacia Synnestvedt, saying that she had clients she was unable to help as well.

I learned a valuable lesson about not trying to work with a client without my guides in attendance. I was reminded that I by myself am not the healer. I am a conduit and the healing is up to my guides.

Going Global

During meditation, Archangel Michael came and flew with me overhead. I heard voices of beings calling out for the stories that I was writing. Michael said, *"They're calling for your message."*

I said, *"The other day they were calling out that they didn't want to hear my message."*

He said, **"Yes, some people will want to hear your message and some people won't."**

Then I heard a deep male voice speaking. He wanted to access my writing, but his words were not in English. It sounded like he was speaking French or another European language. I realized that there are folks who may want to hear my message, but they don't speak English. I knew then that my work was not complete and would reach farther than just in the United States.

Blessing from God

During meditation, I checked in with my guides. I saw Archangel Michael, Divine Mother, Archangels Gabriel, Cassiel, Uriel, Metatron, and Raphael. I met up with my higher self, Mi. Together, we ran up to the immense energy light of God. I soon realized that Mi was escorting me to God.

We fell on our knees at God's feet and bowed our heads. I saw Christ to my left standing and facing God. With my head still bowed, I put out my hand to Christ. He walked to me and took my hand. We continued to face God and Mi took my other hand. I was overcome with emotion and cried softly. God began to speak to me.

You are a child of God. You are a true child of God, recognizing me as your father.

It was difficult for me to stay kneeling under such energy. Still, in energetic form, I bent forward, put my hands on the floor, palms down out in front of me.

Rise up.

I rose back to a kneeling position and turned my face directly to the light of God. I felt loving, divine light on my face and throughout my body.

I love you, God.

I love you, child.

I felt like I was being infused with love.

If you haven't ever felt love, it is difficult to love someone else. The more love that is in you, the more you can share with others. People will sense it in you.

I glowed white, matching God's love. I could not sense my body or even any cells separating my soul from the divine loving light. I was one with the divine, bright light of God. I no longer sensed Mi or Jesus with me.

The distractions of the world will always be there. Focus on my love and light. It will always serve as a home for you.

I saw and felt nature.

Find your playground and your home in nature.

I saw Divine Mother.

She is your mother as I am your father. Be reverent to her; hold her in reverence.

Yes, I love her. I am not worthy.

Don't stay small.

I watched as energy expanded outwards in every direction from my being.

You are a space of infinite possibilities. Your reach is endless. Your reach and therefore, your books' reach are endless.

I saw my arms and energy up as if I was a beacon. It was a much broader beacon than I had seen before. I was stretching my arms out to my sides in all directions.

That is the reach of the book. Endless.

Receive it when it happens and know that all is in divine order. Don't crawl back into your smallness, out of fear or lack of worthiness. You have been divinely created, divinely nurtured, and divinely guided. You listened and acted. This is divinely inspired.

I came back into my angel form, still holding hands with Mi and Jesus.

I love you, God, I love you, Mi and Jesus. I love you, Divine Mother.

Mi escorted me back into my body and the room with my guides. They all laid a hand on me in blessing. I know they are supporting me and that we are all on the same path working together.

The Ministry on the Air

When Spirit suggests I take on a new project, for the most part, I say yes. After the release of my first book, Spirit suggested I talk about it on the radio. Within months, I had lined up a dozen guest spots on radio podcasts. Spirit then encouraged me to host a recurring radio podcast of my own. Soon after that, I was preparing for my own show on the International Angels Network.

I would like to say that I was comfortable and eloquent during my first shows, but that was hardly the case. I was pushing myself to take on the shows, even though before and during each show I was anxious, my heart pounded in my chest, and I had a dry mouth. Spirit brought me so far out of my comfort zone, but I steadfastly trudged ahead. If no one listened, all the better, as I could use that preparation and delivery as a means for practicing for whatever else might be coming my way.

My response to the stress was to be as prepared, in control, and organized as possible. My perfectionistic tendencies surfaced every time, and I would like to think that I was my own worst critic. One morning, I woke up and was immediately planning my radio show in my head. Who knows, maybe I worked on it in my sleep. I sat with my guides during meditation, and they ushered me right up to sit in the presence of One Love. I gladly went. As soon as I got there, my outer skin and all of the worldly trappings, my body, my layers of fear and perfectionism melted away. All that was left was me in soul form with God. I felt great relief and finally, the ability to exhale.

I heard the words, **"Soul to soul. Just speak with them soul to soul."** That I can do.

Channeled from the Divine Mother through Sumaya O'Grady, Excerpts from "Communicating with Divine Mother," Walking with Spirit Radio Podcast, International Angels Network, August 2, 2018

Ruth: Our network, International Angels Network is a pretty new network. It has only been in place about a year and three months. I would like to know on behalf of Claudia Ibarra, the founder, how can we as the hosts and Claudia help International Angels Network to grow?

Sumaya: Beloved Mother Mary, do you have something to share about Ruth's question?

Yes, Ruth, because of the light that you are spreading, and all of the blessings that are coming to you through doing the work that you are doing, you must trust that as you expand your own light, that your shows, that your offerings will reach more people. That much of this is about your believing and trusting in this and seeing it as a reality. I suggest that you and Claudia, your producer, get together and envision where you see this show going because you are both creators. You are both people who have a great vision and a divine mission. As the two of you, and any other parties who you feel are appropriate, join with you envisioning this and seeing it in as much detail as you can, this will take you so much farther faster.

Yes, of course, the ordinary things that you do here on earth, you are very skilled and knowledgeable about these things. But this advice is really from the realm of the soul and who you are as a soul. And what you have to give and how you can expand that by expanding what you see and what is possible. Blessed be.

Sumaya: There is much divine support for what you do and know that. That's very important. Mother Mary is just concluding that she is saying, *"Yes"* that she wants you to know that… and to believe that, to see that, and to feel it.

FIRE

Shortly after the radio show with Sumaya, I sat in meditation. I took note of who was there: Archangel Michael, Divine Mother, Archangel Gabriel, Archangel Uriel, Archangels Cassiel and Metatron and a new figure. It looked like a flame or fire. I started a conversation with Archangel Michael.

Is this an archangel?
No.
Is it ok to work with it?
Yes.
Is it an angel?
Yes.
Is it Fire?

Yes.

Does it represent strength?

Yes.

Fortitude?

Yes.

Power?

Yes.

Are these things that I can be infused with?

Yes.

Can my projects be infused with it?

No.

I shared my fears of being rejected for my work and beliefs. I said that there were times it would be easy for me to walk away from it all. I didn't mind being stretched beyond my comfort zone, but I was now physically and emotionally exhausted. Even this far into my journey, I had my fears that I was wrong, that all the archangels were fakes and I had been duped. Worse than that, I feared I had led others into believing something that wasn't true.

I said, "*I need proof that they are who they say they are.*"

Then each of the guides in front of me turned into my worst nightmare version of themselves. Archangel Michael flew me off and tried to seduce me, Divine Mother turned her back on me, and Archangel Metatron enslaved me and made me work harder and faster. Obviously, these visions represented the shadow side that I feared might be masquerading as the Spiritual Divinity. I turned to Christ, my true North. He was directly in front of God's light. My only true North.

I held the shadow beings aside and stood directly in front of God. The light was so intense it knocked me backward off of my feet. It enveloped me. I saw that the archangels and Divine Mother were back to themselves and were glowing. They were becoming taller, their energy reaching up toward God. Was my energy reaching up and taller as well? Yes. A green tree sprouted out of my head and grew taller, reaching upward to God. It morphed into a tree of life, growing tall, full, and broad with many branches and leaves. God began speaking to me.

The branches and leaves represent everyone that you can lead to me through your stories.

Is the journey through Christ?

No.

Is it direct to you?

Yes.

Are my books about knowing Christ?

No.

Are my books about knowing God?

Yes. You are Christlike.

No, I'm not.

You are human trying to lead people to me.

Did you say that people need to come to you through Christ?

No.

Did Christ say that people need to come to you through him?

No.

Did man say that people need to come to you through Christ?

Yes.

God, should I keep working in the same direction and with the same beings that I am?

Yes.

Is there anything else?

Yes. I love you.

I love you.

There was a large explosion of God's energy that knocked me off my feet. I felt peace and a renewed sense of direction. I thought, "I don't need to justify myself or anything, but just keep moving forward."

Baptized by Fire

The next morning, I was met by the same Spiritual Divinity and Fire. I hadn't been taught anything by Fire yet. So, why was she here? I positioned my body to be facing Fire directly. The Holy Spirit began to speak.

Baptism by Fire.

I felt shudders throughout my body as I released and shifted energy. I was grateful for the healing, so I went to hug Fire. She moved away as if she was vapor.

Can I ask you some questions?

No.

I fell to my knees and thanked God for this baptism by Fire. But, what did this all mean? I saw a vision of my oldest daughter getting her wisdom teeth out. She was quite fearful for the upcoming surgery.

We will be with her; she will be fine.

Was I just baptized by the Holy Spirit?

No.

Was I baptized in the Holy Spirit?

Yes.

Will I have more power now?

I was not sure what I meant by "power." I was expecting to hear "no."

Yes.

Will I have more power to heal?

No.

To teach?

No.

To reach others?

Yes/no.

As I am a minister, can I baptize people?

No.

Saint.

Does being baptized in the Holy Spirit give me some sort of title like Saint?

Yes.

I wasn't quite sure what to do with that answer so I asked again.

Yes.

The archangels started clapping, laughing, and cheering. I was overwhelmed and in tears.

Archangel Michael, is this real?

Yes.

Divine Mother, is this real?

Yes.

What does this mean?

Saint means friend of God.

I love that!

I am Ruth, friend of God.

Does being baptized in the Holy Spirit give me more fortitude?

No.

Does it give me more strength to persevere?

Yes.

I bowed in front of the archangels. They laid hands on me and blessed me for the journey ahead.

Is there anything else?

I love you.

I love you too.

7TH HEAVEN

A few days later, I went to sit with God. I found myself at the orange-yellow crystalline wall of One Love. * (*Footnote: For more information on the crystalline healing wall, refer to *One Love: Divine Healing at Open Clinic*, author: Ruth Anderson, SageHouse Press) Interesting, I haven't seen the crystalline healing wall of One Love for quite a while. In body, I experienced many yawns and shifting energy. The orange-yellow color intensified to red. My body felt intensity on my back behind my navel. The healing color turned olive green. I experienced more yawns and shifting energy physically. The olive-green color changed to clear, see-through, light black. My body responded with more yawns and energetic release.

I saw a person's form standing facing me embedded in the rock. I was not afraid, and not feeling emotionally connected to the form; I didn't imagine it represented me. The person was not moving.

Is that a prehistoric man?

No.

Maybe it was representing me after all.

Is that me?

Yes.

Is that me in the past?

No.

Is that me now?

No.

Is that me in the future?

Yes.

I thought it looked somewhat masculine.

Is it male?

No.

Is it female?

No.

Are those angel wings?

Yes.

I remembered that angels help people on Earth or in the Cathedral of Souls.

Will I be helping people on Earth?
No.
Will I be stuck in this rock?
I smiled.
No.
Will I be helping people on Earth?
No.
Will I be in the Cathedral of Souls?
No.
Will I be in Heaven?
No.
Will I be with you?
Yes.
Nice!
Does my angel in the rock stay there all of the time?
No.
Is that just there for my learning?
Yes.
Will we be in the 7th Heaven?
Yes.
Cool, I needed to read up on that.
What can other people do to get to 7th Heaven?
Know me and love me. 7th Heaven is reserved for those that I am closest to, family.
I saw myself now sitting at the feet of God.
I love my family dearly. I want them to be with me.
Then teach them to know me and love me.
I saw Mi sitting there with us. She was chatting with God as if she was with a long-lost friend. It was the black-haired Mi, not the blond curly long hair Mi. When did my hair change color, length, and straightness?

God, if my higher self wasn't that close to you, would I be going to 7th Heaven?

No. Righteous Servant.

Did you say she was a righteous servant?

Yes.

When I heard "Saint, Friend of God," was that written about my higher self?

Yes.

Was that written about Mi?

Yes.

Was that written about me?

Yes.

Is that when my hair changed color?

Yes.

This version of Mi looked more serious, intent, purposeful. The earlier blonde Mi seemed content to dance with her friends and less driven.

It is easy to change appearance here.

Did Mi's appearance change as a result of my changing?

Yes. As you became more focused, driven, you saw a need for the change.

Did I become more in alignment with her?

Yes.

I love Mi.

You are Mi.

Mi and I merged as one.

Is there anything else?

Love one another as I have loved you.

I checked in with my guides. I saw not only my guides but a great number of souls out of body lined up and milling around.

Are you all waiting for this book?

Yes.

It was a friendly reminder that I have an audience in the ethereal realm.

Channeled by Karen Anderson
Spiritual Intuitive, Medium and Teacher

My dear friend and fellow lightworker emailed me information that she had seen on my behalf. [Bold and italics mine.]

"Hi, sweet Ruth, when I first checked in with your angels, there was a huge heart encircling you, them, and the world. What a sight to see, I was fascinated and wanted to see more. They are preparing you for the World to know of your work and the book, (the first one), is a door opener. The projects and more books that will come will bust the door wide open. The clearing of your personal time, is more of a structured way to give you more hours in the day to concentrate on the new and what is to leave or fizzle out, will. You will always be in service to humankind; it is now beginning to take on different roots and will grow exponentially as time moves forward.

"What you have been preparing for has been all of the moments, years, and experiences shared with your Angelic and Galactic Team to bring higher messages to many hearts that are open to hear, feel, and know their own power within. Many who come to you have been assigned well before either of you contracted to this Earth Life. It is more of a timing, and now the timing has begun.

"Here is a message from your Angelic/Galactic Team: **Child of Light, Precious One, be not afraid of the tasks ahead that you are undertaking. In fear we mean, overwhelmed of the enormity of the process or the feel of it. You are not alone, never have you ever been,** *nor ever will you be. We have assembled together so many key play-ers on Earth and in the Universe to bring the Mastery that is you and many others forward. Let the unfolding be, one petal at a time, as a delicate flower opens to the Sun. Let the 'Central Sun,' i.e. Source, be your guide child. Many of the puzzle pieces are coming together to re-ceive the greater picture. You began this by leaping and trusting what you are receiving. Continue to leap, faithfully into the next piece that is given.*

"You are meant for this position, you have always been meant for this position as it is you that holds the golden ray of truth through-out the ages that opens hearts to all that meet you. Ask us into your meditations to continue to inspire, enlighten you and those around you. And, you shall be as well enlightened by those who come to you.

"We see many teachers, masters, ready to stand as a Super Consciousness Community where many will come, bring their truths, share their truths, and many will be enlightened as if your light is igniting many others' lights. We see this happening all over the world with many Masters coming forward and bringing their leadership to the forefront. We applaud you, we thank you, we are blessed to see you have said YES to all that Spirit, Source, and Self (God/Goddess Self) have brought to your human consciousness.

"Continue to breathe child, continue to adjust your frequencies to the new and uplifting information. You will always be carried and supported, never burdened by this wonderful mission that is ahead. With great love, respect, and honor, we leave you this message through beloved channel known as Karen. Go, child. Ignite the flame of higher consciousness to expand in to every corner of this planet and out into the Universe."

chapter eighteen

Connection to Spirit

Several times when I have gone to see the Spiritual Divinity, sit in meditation, or to prepare my space for a client, I sat down and started to go through my ritual: feet flat on the floor, sitting up, ground myself, run my energy, etc. I have seen the Divinity standing there as if waiting for me. I heard, ***"You don't need to do that."*** And I knew that they were correct. I was already in connection with them, as evidenced by the fact that they were already there talking to me. My connection is not about posture, chants, incantations, or rituals. It is about being still; opening my heart, soul, and mind; and welcoming spirit to spirit communication.

Channeled Excerpts from the Divine Mother through Sumaya O'Grady Walking with Spirit Radio Podcast, International Angels Network, August 9, 2018

Ruth: Do you mind asking her how can people connect with the Spiritual Divinity? I know whenever I have thought "Oh, I need to make sure I use these words, or be sitting in this posture to be able to connect," I am always reminded, "You don't need to do that." So, I would love to hear from Divine Mother what the best way for people to try to connect with her is?

Sumaya: I can feel her smiling right now, and she has kind of like an energetic chuckle.

Yes, Beloveds, there is no formula that you need to be concerned about. It is most important to just take some private time. If you can get a little bit of silence, it does not have to be long, to sit down somewhere and to take in some breaths. Because you always have your breath with you. And to really just give yourself the time to breathe, to really just inhale and exhale consciously and to feel your breath flowing through your body. And then know when you breathe like that, that that allows you to access your heart. And this is not particularly a formula, this is something that I am suggesting and you can adapt it to any way that you feel guided to. That you may place your hand over your heart and connect with that part of you that is divine.

And just say, "I am a divine being. I am a being of love. I am guided." Use any phrases like that that come to you.

If you are looking for abundance, say, "I am divine abundance." Anything like that. If you are looking for peace, say, "I am divine peace." And then, as you choose, this is very, very simple, and there is really no formula, but to really just tap into your own heart, and ask whatever question. Because when you are connecting to yourself, as a divine being, you can ask that question and you will receive an answer.

You will always receive an answer. Although, the answer may come to you as a feeling or as a knowing, it may not always come in the form of skywriting or in the form of advice spoken into your ear. But to trust that the wisdom is dropped into your heart, that the knowing of what to do is something that's already within you. It is not really outside of you. It is important that you know that and that you trust that.

And that is my advice to you. And the more you do this, the easier this will become, and the more able you will be to trust. To trust yourself and to trust your ability to hear divine wisdom, to trust your knowingness of you as a divine being. This is the most important part. And this will also prepare you for all the ups and downs of things that the world is going through now. As you tap into your own divinity and the more you do this, throughout the day, on a daily basis, as often as you can, for two minutes or five minutes or an hour, whatever you can do. Do not feel put upon by a formula. This is very flexible, you can use what I have said as just a simple example, because you always have your breath. And that's one way that you can tap in. To cover your heart and say hello. Breath into your heart and connect deeply into that. And just know that you are home. That is my answer to your question. Blessed be.

The Gift of Life

I start my meditation time by sitting with God, or what I refer to as "sitting at the feet of God." One morning as I sat in God's presence, I waited for any words, feelings, or visions that I might be lucky enough to witness. Nope, nothing. I tried to fill the silence.

Will you heal my mouth?

For a month I had been acutely aware of tremors in my mouth that were transitory and seemed heightened by stress.

NO!

Well then, will you fix my hair loss?

My grandmother's early hair thinning had been passed down to me. The answer was not one that I expected.

You say I don't do miracles, so, why would I do one for you?

True, in my earlier book I had written about God and miracles.

I wrote that I think people distance themselves from you when they ask for a miracle, and it doesn't happen. I said that some people have unrealistic expectations of you, seeing you as a Santa Claus figure in the sky. I said go ahead and pray for a miracle. I said don't expect a miracle to happen all the time, because that is why they are called miracles. Sometimes they happen.

But, why pray for a miracle if you don't have faith that it will happen?

Good point.

I ask that people have the smallest faith, like that of the grain of a mustard seed.

So, are you saying that people whose prayers weren't answered didn't have enough faith that the prayer would be answered?

Some.

And others?

What they prayed for wasn't in their life plans.

Do you hear every prayer?

I surely expected the answer to be yes.

No.

Well, maybe this is done by proxy.

Do the angels hear every prayer?

No.

A prayer from someone who does not believe in me will not be heard.

Do some people ever have a miracle and then start believing in you?

No.

Love; it's about love. A child doesn't think, "I am going to love my parent in order to get a present." They simply love their parent and

the parent in turn wants to give them presents out of love, out of delight, for the closeness they share.

So, is the problem that people come to you solely for what they can get from you?

Yes.

It is the conversations; the time spent communing together that fosters a loving connection. If a miracle were to happen, wouldn't you think that it would be for someone who already knows me and loves me?

And then is it a miracle or merely a gift of love?

(No answer.)

That time with me, listening and sharing, that is the gift of life.

I felt a yellow-orange light healing coming from One Love and moving throughout my body. I remembered yellow-orange as the chakra colors of my I Am, that which is my life's purpose, that which makes my heart beat. I felt a quenching of the thirst of my soul. I thought of Qi, the life force energy that pulses through each of us.

Is your healing for each person that knows you, your "gift of life," feeding their pinpoint of color from the I Am, tailored to their soul and what it needs?

Yes.

You came to me for hair loss; I gave you the gift of life. Is that what you asked for? No. Is that what your soul craves? Yes.

The desires of the ego versus the cravings of the soul. Which do you think I value more?

But when someone prays fervently for a loved one to survive...?

That is for me to work with the two souls, the one petitioning and the other who is facing death. It is specific to them; I can't answer that for you.

Of course.

Spend more time with me; I will tell you more.

Thank you.

I smiled, as this was not said just to me but anyone reading these words.

I left feeling full of yellow-orange healing light, that which my soul craves and makes my heart beat. The gift of life.

Holy Communion

I liken prayer to time spent in conversation with my creator. I interviewed Dr. Nancy Tarr Hart on my radio podcast, and we were discussing her lifelong relationship with Divine Mother. I asked Nancy if she spent time in prayer daily, meditated, or simply had open lines of communication with the Spiritual Divinity much of the time. As I asked the question, I thought, "What a silly question." What kind of relationship thrives on setting aside 15 minutes every few days for shared communication? I can't fathom going to my daughters and stating, "Ok, I have time to talk with you now and Wednesday for 15 minutes. Other than that, I won't be talking with you or thinking of you for the rest of the week. Start now!"

I was shown a new definition of "Holy Communion." Maybe it is merely the time we each spend communing with God.

Hey, Spirit

I was driving across town and wanted to text my daughter to tell her I was running a few minutes late. I picked up my phone and prepared to dictate my message to Siri, the automated concierge for Apple cell phones. But instead of saying "Hey, Siri" to activate the dictation feature, I called out, "Hey, Spirit." I laughed out loud when I realized my mistake. But really, that's what it's like for me. I close my eyes and ask for the Divinity to be there; within minutes, oftentimes seconds, they appear.

INTERCESSION

I sat in meditation with God. Our conversation started with one word from God.

Intercession.

I know that intercession means the act of praying with someone else in mind. I saw a vision of my oldest daughter. Sometimes she struggles with preparing for tests. We hired a tutor who seemed demanding, and my daughter wasn't sure what she thought of him.

Is her teacher the right one for her?

Yes.

I thought of her AP Language Arts class and how she is wondering if it was the right course for her.

Can I ask you about her AP LA class?

NO! That's where prayer comes in. Pray about it.

So, I should pray to you about her making the right choice for her LA class?

Yes.

So now my brain went to someone I had contracted to help me with a project.

Am I supposed to be thinking about that person right now?

Yes.

I am very frustrated. I would like to get that project completed.

Pray about it.

So, it's ok to pray about things that might otherwise seem trivial?

Yes, say what's on your mind. As you tell me about other people, you are praying for them.

Intercession. Intercession is making someone else's needs more important than your own.

Is intercession always prayer?

No.

By putting someone else first through your time and service, is that intercession?

Yes.

Curious, I looked up the definition of intercession. It read: the action of intervening on behalf of another through mediation, arbitration, negotiation, and diplomacy. The definition also includes the action of saying a prayer on behalf of another person.

I saw a vision of Divine Mother.

Are you showing me that intercession is one of the many faces of Divine Mother?

Yes.

When you say that, do you mean both kinds of intercession, both prayer and interceding with someone else?

Yes. Start your day with intercession. When you pray, pray with others in mind. Tell me your concerns for them. I will listen. Even if the person doesn't know me in their heart, I will listen.

I checked on what I had heard earlier.

Will you listen to the pleas of those who don't believe in you?

No.

But you will listen to the prayers of someone who doesn't know you because that is how someone gets to know you?

Yes.

Is that why people say you didn't answer prayers because they don't know you or believe in you and all they did was ask for requests?

Yes.

When someone who knows you asks for a request, do they have a better chance at having a request accepted?

Yes.

That makes sense.

Should people who know you be seen as having special value because you listen to them on behalf of others?

Yes.

Might that value equate to financial gain? In other words, would it be ok for someone to accept payment for praying on someone else's behalf?

No.

Does that value mean they should be held in higher esteem?

Yes.

Should the person doing the praying hold themselves in higher esteem?

No.

LISTENING WITH ONE EAR OPEN

I write a recurring newspaper column for the Shelton Mason County Journal, a weekly newspaper for 8,000 subscribers in Shelton Mason County which is in Washington State near Seattle. I woke up the other morning thinking about options for topics for my next journal entry. As I got dressed, I had the idea of trying to syndicate my column to newspapers across the country, but in retrospect, I think I was given the idea.

Once I was ready for the day, I went into my office to meditate. I immediately sensed the presence of some of my guides. Saint Francis was the first spirit that I identified, followed by an Archangel who guides me with finances, Archangel Gabriel, Divine Mother, and lastly, Archangel Michael. I dove right into our conversations.

Earlier this morning, I heard that I should syndicate my newspaper columns. Did I hear that from one of you?

Yes.

Who did I hear that from? Archangel Michael, Did I hear that from you?

Yes.

Divine Mother?

Yes.

Archangel Gabriel, did I hear that from you, too?

Yes.

My mouth was agape at the idea of all three guides offering me advice that I hadn't asked for. Then I wanted to know exactly how that happened and I wasn't aware of it.

Did you all say it at the same time?

No.

Did I hear it three different times?

Yes.

I knew I had heard it once when I was awake, but when were the other two?

Did I hear it from some of you when I was sleeping?

Yes.

Archangel Michael, did you tell me when I was awake?

No.

Did you tell me when I was sleeping?

Yes.

Did you show me in a dream?

Yes.

Divine Mother, did you tell me when I was awake?

Yes.

So, that must have been the guidance I heard while I was getting dressed.

Archangel Gabriel, did you tell me when I was awake?

No.

Did you tell me when I was sleeping?

Yes.

Did you tell me in a dream?

No.

Did you simply say it to me?

Yes.

I know I receive information in dreams; that has happened so many times. But this feels different somehow.

Do you guys do that? Archangel Michael, do you just tell me things in my sleep?

Yes.

Divine Mother, do you just tell me things in my sleep?

Yes.

Wow! I thought that I needed to meditate or be consciously tuned in to receive guidance. Although when I think about it, I know that I have received guidance at times when I am not meditating. But this feels so intentional on their part; to tell me things while I am sleeping. I was stunned.

Am I that important to you that you come to talk to me in my sleep?

Yes.

Tears came to my eyes. I wondered how long this had been going on.

Archangel Michael, did you ever talk to me in my sleep before I started really learning about intuition?

No.

Divine Mother?

No.

Archangel Gabriel?

No.

Archangel Gabriel, did I hear your words while I was sleeping last night?

Yes.

Archangel Michael, did I hear it when you showed it to me in a dream?

Yes.

Divine Mother, did I hear it when you told it to me when I was awake?

No.

Ouch.

Archangel Gabriel, is that why you told me while I was asleep because I miss things when Divine Mother says them?

Yes.

Archangel Michael, is that why you showed me in a dream?

Yes.

Divine Mother, I am so sorry I didn't hear you. Yours must be a small, still voice because all I did was get up and get ready. Oh. Wait a minute. I laid in bed for 10 minutes first checking emails and then Facebook. Was I distracted by something else when you told me?

Yes.

I would like to know what I was doing and didn't hear you. Was I still lying in bed when you told me?

Yes.

Was I looking at my phone?

No.

Was I looking at my computer?

Yes.

Gulp. Who else have I not heard because I was nose down looking at a computer screen? My thoughts went to my kids.

Was I looking at emails?

Yes.

Was I on Facebook?

No. I thought first thing in the morning was our time before the world crept in.

Yes, absolutely, the world can wait. Divine Mother, I hate to ask, but have I missed your saying other things to me?

Yes.

Is it because I was on the computer at the time?

Yes.

Is it because I was watching TV?

No.

I didn't think so, because I so rarely watch TV.

Archangel Michael, have I missed you saying things to me because I was on the computer?

No.

Archangel Gabriel, how about you?

No.

A small still voice. Divine Mother, thank you for wanting to connect with me during the day when I am not even thinking of connecting with you. That is pretty humbling. I will be more aware of slowing down and finding quiet with no distractions, so I can be listening for that small, still voice. I love you.

Channeled from the Divine Mother through Danielle Nistor, Excerpts from "Connection with the Divine Mother for Healing, Guidance and Divine Love," Walking with Spirit Radio Podcast, International Angels Network, October 11, 2018

Ruth: Does Divine Mother have anything she would like to share with the listening audience?

Danielle: So, it's something that comes to me very strongly about you, which is a book for little children with prayers, with messages, with encouragement, and it may be, and I see it with very, very beautiful pictures inside. What I'm getting as a visual is, unfortunately, it may be that this is to be addressed to children in the hospital, because I see a little girl with her head completely bald. I hear like those strong problems, illnesses for which they may need understanding somehow like, I don't know, maybe leukemia or cancer. This is what is coming to me. For you to create some support, some soothing for their souls. I see lots of butterflies connected with this book and these children, which I'm not sure what the message is.

Ruth: I can tell you what the message is. Spirit will use butterflies sometimes to send me messages, whether it's support for writing a book, or healing of a loved one, or the death of my mother-in-law. It is typically yellow butterflies, so I understand that.

Danielle: Well, wonderful! Thank God you like writing, and you are a messenger and a person with an open, loving heart. For your audience, that's interesting because now they show me that you have an interesting audience: younger ladies, mature ladies, some men. It seems like they are looking for the pure water. They are coming to a well with a desire to feed their hearts, their souls, and as a way to remember. And the message that I get is that for them to spend time with themselves in the intimacy of their home with their hands on the heart, inviting the true essence, their own truth, to speak to them. To do this on their own, to do this during the time when they listen to your show. And then just open to hear whatever it is between the lines that is addressing exactly what they need to hear, what they need to receive at this time in their life.

Also, the remembrance that there are legions of angels serving our planet and they need, they are waiting for us to call on them. It is their joy to support us. But it needs to come from us, this invitation. Otherwise, they will support us only in a very dramatic situation like life or death. Of course, the divine embrace of the Divine Mother who is above all of us is sending stars from her beautiful eyes, stars of love, the most beautiful blue light and rays of pinkish purple love are going to each of us in our hearts. But that wound that is ready to be healed, be closed, which is usually about our mother, our own mother. So, the Divine Mother is coming as the Divine Mother who wants to heal us with our earthly mother. And the reassurance that we are innocent, whole, and complete, and deeply loved no matter what is the situation and the circumstances in our lives right now. And I am complete and she says her goodbye to us. Leaving us being enfolded in her love, her grace.

Ruth: Thank you so much, Danielle. Thank you so much, Divine Mother. I have a question. You mentioned sending stars of love from her eyes, and I have seen so many times, stars. I have been told several times that stars are a gift of love from God and that they bring gifts of light into the darkness. I have seen stars repeatedly in meditation and receiving blessings. So, I think it's fascinating that you were seeing stars coming from her eyes. Is that a common symbol for you?

Danielle: Not at all. Actually, it looks like they are talking your language. For me, it's the first time that I have seen such a thing. It was so beautiful, like sparkles. Beautiful blue sparkling coming out from her eyes which is the first time in my life when I have this vision.

Ruth: Well, I am quite honored and they were speaking my language as evidenced by the butterflies and then the stars. It is so rewarding to have that validation, and not that I was needing validation, but to get validation just as a gift of, "Yes, the things that you are seeing are the same things that Danielle is seeing because we are sending it to you." So, that's beautiful, so thank you so much.

Danielle: We are so, so blessed to have such an exquisite theme of angelic divine beings who are doing everything possible, so we can get it.

WHAT'S IN A NAME?

One morning several months back, I had an uneasy feeling. As the day progressed, the angst in my gut continued to build until my tears were falling. I couldn't explain my discomfort, and my attempts to calm myself were futile. I took a hot shower to relax. In the shower, a large wave of panic came over me. I sobbed and gasped for breath. Having never had a panic attack before, I was simultaneously intrigued and overcome with emotion. I called on my guides but felt no one there. I knew that this was my moment to stand alone with my body, emotions, and spirit. This was my time to fall completely apart in order to rebuild a stronger, more substantial version of myself. I had never felt so vulnerable. Yet, once I had made my way through to the other side of it, I had never felt so invincible.

A few days ago, I awoke in the morning with that now familiar discomfort in the pit of my stomach. Was I going to be heading off again into another panic attack? I remembered the panic attack I had in the shower. I decided to ask Archangel Michael about it.

Was that panic attack because my soul knew all that would be coming up in my life plan?

Yes.

Was that panic attack my body needing to catch up with how far my soul had come and where I would be heading?

Yes.

Is this panic I am now feeling just because I am remembering that last panic attack?

No.

Is this panic because my soul knows how far my world will change with all that is coming before me?

No.

Is this fear because I am sensing danger?

No.

With this panic, am I merely releasing energy that no longer serves me?

No.

Is this fear because I know that I need to come home to spend more time with the Spiritual Divinity?

No.

Is my panic my body trying to catch up to my spirit?

No.

Even though I was not receiving clarity, I felt calmer and was no longer triggered.

I am getting a lot of, "Nos." Is anyone listening? Archangel Michael, are you there?

There was no answer

God, are you there?

No answer

Is anyone there?

No answer

Is that my big fear, that no one is listening?

No.

So, I just reached out to no one because I didn't specify who I was reaching out to. Right?

Yes.

Is this a lesson for me to know and tell others that we need to specify which of the Spiritual Divinity we wish to connect with?

Yes.

HOT NEW RELEASES

When creating the cover for my second book, I was told I could use the phrase "international bestselling author," because two anthologies that I have chapters in received international bestselling status on Amazon. I didn't feel comfortable using that term as my chapter was just one of many. So, I was hoping beyond hope that my second book could achieve International Bestselling status. As the only author, then I could embrace the term, feeling like I had indeed earned it.

My second book, *Walking with Spirit: Divine Illuminations on Life, Death, and Beyond* launched August 2018 on Amazon. In less than five hours, it reached the status of a bestseller for the category of Angels, and overnight it became an international bestseller. I was ecstatic! Finally, the messages that Spirit had impressed upon my heart to put out into the world were being acknowledged. On the Amazon site, while a book is ranking as an international bestseller, an orange banner is placed next to the book cover announcing the achievement. I proudly took several photos of the computer screen with my book cover emblazoned with the orange banner. I was excited that I could finally put the words "international best-selling" on the paperback version of my book.

I went into meditation and saw angels dancing, waving the Amazon orange banner. It was quite a celebration! The angels were so excited, and it felt like an acknowledgment that this book would be able to reach the hearts of many and share how people could connect with the angels and Divinity! The next day in meditation, my higher self and I sat in God's presence, and Mi proudly presented God with the orange banner. There was celebration all around.

I told my cover designer that I would welcome the words "international bestseller" on my book cover now that I had really earned it. Weeks later, I learned how to access the sales reports. My heart plummeted when I saw that my time as international bestselling author only resulted in the sale of 60 books. Could that be? I have learned that there are algorithms that Amazon employs to determine what is selling like hotcakes within a given timeframe. My book sold 60 copies within a short period. When one person in the UK and two people in Australia purchased my book during that period, it catapulted it to international bestseller status.

I didn't feel right about the sale of 60 books earning the title of international bestselling author. While devastated might be too strong of a word, I was clearly dealing with an ethical dilemma. Should I embrace the title or not? I didn't want to try and fool anyone or come across as something that I wasn't. I went into meditation. I was reminded of the angels that danced and celebrated, waving the orange banner and the celebration when my higher self presented it to God. There had been a celebration that was created by the angels, not by me. Who was I to say that the angels had been wrong or foolish? As I sat with that thought, something slowly dawned on me. What if the angels were actually instrumental in some of those books selling so that the book reached international bestselling status? I didn't know all of the buyers, and definitely not the ones in the UK or Australia. What if the angels whispered in someone's ear and suggested they buy my book? What if I reached 60 buyers <u>because</u> of the angels' support? Who am I to snub the whispering of the angels? Clearly, the sale of 60 books resulted in the angels dancing and embracing the title with my higher self. Who am I to turn down this gift, this acknowledgment? So, I decided to embrace the title of International Bestselling Author, and in so doing, I am winking toward the heavens.

Section Six

Enlighten

chapter nineteen

Warrior for God

In meditation, I was shown an immensely large angel. In earthly terms, I would say their height was about six stories tall. I asked why the angel was so huge. I heard it was for my protection. I asked God what in the world I was getting myself involved with that I would need this much protection. Apparently, it was a rhetorical question, as I received no answer.

ENLIGHTENED WORLD

Archangel Michael worked overtime in order to impress upon me the need to come forward and make a positive change in the world. Like so many others, I was acutely aware of an increase in negativity, fear, hatred, and all of the isms (like racism) that led to isolation and an "us against them mentality." I was guided to start what was called "A

Renaissance of One." I started a Facebook campaign and did what I could to share positive, inclusive and encouraging messages.

Over time, I was shown the need to bring others together in order to have a larger reach and a greater impact. Embodying a spiritual positive movement on behalf of humanity and the planet was going to need more than just me. Over months of daily meditation, Archangel Michael shared details with me about an enterprise called Enlightened World. I was urgently being requested to orchestrate it and share it with the world. I did my best to follow the guidance that was shown me.

As I had conversations with others about Enlightened World, I understood that many other lightworkers had been given huge to-do lists from Spirit as well, all with the same sense of urgency. Obviously, Enlightened World was part of a much larger spirit-led movement to assist humankind now.

I have been called, as many of you have been, to share the truth that Spirit and the Universe have laid on my heart. We all know that planet Earth and her inhabitants are struggling more now than ever. I believe that what could make this situation more bearable, would be for people to have hope, connection, and purpose. I have been shown that the time to act is now, and I have answered the call along with other lightworkers.

I conjecture that lightworkers across the globe are being isolated and distracted from reaching as many individuals as possible. I believe that lower level entities don't want humanity to reach the highest levels of consciousness possible and are keeping lightworkers distracted with politics, current events, technology and the demands of creating businesses. Sadly, this comes at a time when we most need positivity and expanded consciousness.

Part of my calling is to create a network, a platform, and a voice for lightworkers across the globe to unite in many ways so ultimately, they can have a much larger reach and impact. The goal is to assist lightworkers in increasing the vibrational frequencies of one, and of many, who can then present a united front across the globe to counter the lower level energies of fear, hatred and the exclusionary isms. Ultimately, lightworkers can assist individuals in discovering connection with the divine light and the spiritual divinity.

I was given a name for this endeavor: Enlighten. I was guided to use the domain name www.enlightenedworld.online and the Facebook group Enlightened World Unites. Listening to Archangel Michael, I reached out to Rebecca Hall Gruyter of RHGTV Network. She graciously accepted Enlightened World Network (EWN) as the newest member of her online TV programming Network. EWN, an online network for spiritually transformational programs, serves to support lightworkers who are reticent to commit to creating weekly podcasts, but want to start out with a more manageable number of episodes.

Www.enlightenedworld.online supports lightworkers by providing support for building professional visibility such as submitting articles, advertising and connecting with contractors for technical and marketing support. In addition, on the website, members are encouraged to spend time in prayer and meditation with others on behalf of humanity, nature and the planet. Our goals are to raise levels of consciousness, increase awareness of the planet, hope to help people become aware of the changes they can individually make that will support earth and all its inhabitants, make connections with the spiritual divinity, and free up lightworkers to spend time working with individuals using the skills and gifts of bringing in divine light to the world. Please check out both www.enlightenedworld.online and www.enlightenedworldnetwork.com and find a sanctuary and a place to call home with like-minded individuals across the globe.

God's Army

In meditation several mornings in a row, I saw myself as a participant in God's army. Each soldier was decked out in armor and atop a horse with protective shields and weapons. I asked what the armor was and I was told it was "God's Word." I recognized my friend Denice next to me. I asked Archangel Michael a few questions:

Are the archangels part of God's army?

No.

Are those in God's army all people in bodies?

No.

Is Christ in God's army?

No.

Are any of the biblical figures in God's army?

No.

As I looked around, I saw that there were many knights behind me, but who was in front of me? Surely, we were not the leads. There were many riders in front and on the sides of us. In the very front, four riders stood out as leaders. They did not look similar to the other soldiers, as they were made of light. I heard "***The Four Horsemen.***" I knew that this corresponded with the Four Horsemen of the Apocalypse as described in the book of Revelations. I do not know what this means for those of us on Earth, but I do know that I am pleased to be firmly *behind* the Four Horsemen in God's army, and not facing them from the other side.

I evaluated myself astride the horse, decked out in armor. It was me in the protective armor, not Mi, my higher self. I knew that I had embraced the calling to be a spiritual leader here on Earth, and that had been recognized in the spiritual world as well. Finally, I felt that my work on Earth in body was aligned with the work that Mi was doing in the ethereal realm.

As I looked around, I saw that Denice and I were squarely in the middle of the army. We were well protected from all sides. This brought me some peace of mind about stepping further into the world to share the work that I had been asked to carry forward.

The Power of We

Whenever two or more are gathered in prayer or meditation, there is power beyond measure. -**Divine Mother**

One day, I meditated with a colleague, Cynthia Stott. The experience was profound. I was reminded that when two or more are gathered that there is immense power in prayer and meditation. I encourage each of you to find a partner or a circle of like-minded friends who are willing to sit in meditation or prayer with you. Together we can have a more significant impact on our situation, our lives, and our world. If it only took the selling of 60 books for the angels to dance in the heavens, imagine the impact it could have if many people came together to pray and meditate on behalf of the planet and humankind.

When Two or More Are Gathered

I was asked to lead a meditation for a conference of the International Association of Near-Death Studies. About 12 participants showed up at the early morning get together. I invited the Spiritual Divinity into the room and held space while everyone sat in a circle and started meditating. I noticed the archangels moved to the group; Divine Mother, Archangels Michael, Gabriel, and Raphael stood behind the participants, interspersed evenly around the circle. Soon after that, about 20 angels that were lesser in stature joined in and created a ring around the archangels. A handful of childlike angels called "sprites" joined into the outer band of angels.

In spirit, the participants and I all held our arms up to the creator and rays of light shone upward to the heavens from each person. The archangels and angels held their arms up to God as well. The light rays emanating from them joined with our light rays, creating one larger beam of light reaching up to the heavens. I mentioned the strength in people coming together to meditate or pray. We sat and basked in the energy of praise and connection for a few minutes.

The archangels then turned the energy inward to provide healing and connection to those participants in the room. Again, we sat silently and basked in the healing energy. I heard faint angelic music and mentioned it to the group. Pink angelic flowers appeared at our feet. I announced them and questioned what they symbolized. I heard it was in appreciation and gratitude for the light that each participant shared with the Divinity and would then be able to share with others.

I was presented with an energetic basket of golden flowers and was instructed to stand in front of each person one at a time and hand them a flower. As I did that, if they were comfortable to do so, they were to say their full name out loud. The angels would then share that name with the creator. This was to signify each participant's willingness to be seen and acknowledged in the spirit realm and would provide name or spirit recognition for subsequent meditations.

I made my way around the group members slowly, first asking each one for a name, handing out a "golden flower," and watching as an angel listened to the name and flew upward and relayed the name out loud to the creator. As I slowly worked my way around the circle, this gesture of each person putting their name out to be acknowledged and recognized by the Spiritual Divinity felt to me like a profound moment for each of them as a spiritual being. After each person's name was told to the creator, the name of an archangel or Divine Mother was said to me, and I shared that with the recipient. Participants were encouraged to connect with this spiritual being at a later time through mediation.

I was told to give the group time for each person to seek a private connection with their guide, so I asked each one to call in that guide by name and sit with their energy for a few minutes.

Collectively with the angels, we then sent another vast column of light to the creator. The column of light seemed stronger, brighter, and wider than the first time. After a few minutes, the archangels and angels laid hands on the circle of participants in a gesture of blessing.

I was then directed to walk the group through a healing of the planet Earth. We symbolically and energetically put the Mother Earth in the middle of our circle. The angels and archangels still encircling us joined in our efforts, and together we focused our energy and turned the rays of light coming through our arms and hands to Earth, nature, and lastly, humanity, while we asked for healing, nurturance, love, light, peace, and respite.

Lastly, we expressed gratitude to the angels, archangels, Divine Mother, and the Heavenly Creator.

After the meditation, several of the participants shared their experiences:

One of the women experienced smelling a strong scent of rose, and a second watched as large vats of silver metallic light were poured on us as a group. Another participant, Tiffany, mentioned that she had heard an angelic band and saw a man in a black suit come into the room and sit at a back table and observe. I asked if the gentleman was in spirit or in body. She answered that he was in spirit. I wanted to find out if this new spirit was benevolent or not. I started by asking Archangel Michael if this gentleman's spirit was evil.

No.

I didn't think so, as I had felt only higher vibrational energies throughout the meditation.

Was it of the good?

Yes.

Was this visit somehow crucial to my future work?
Yes.

Man in Black

The next morning in meditation, I saw the figure in black among my lineup of guides. As I watched it, the black suit disappeared and the being turned to vapors.

Archangel Michael, is there anything I need to know about the figure in the black suit?
Yes.
Who was it?
Holy Spirit.
Was that the Holy Spirit?
Yes.

I laughed at the thought of the Holy Spirit in a dress suit looking like a character in Men in Black.

Was the Holy Spirit there to hold space for what I was doing?
No.
Was the Holy Spirit there to watch what I was doing?
Yes.
God, is there anything else?
Yes.
Holy Spirit.
Was it there testing me?
No.
Was it there observing if I would follow the guidance I was being given?
Yes.
To see just how far you could take me?
Yes. You passed.

I felt God smile.
But it wasn't a test, right?
We both smiled.

WHAT YOU NAME, WHAT YOU WANT?

In meditation, I went to sit at God's feet. I was taken to the healing crystalline mass of One Love. The color started out as yellow, with healing to my third chakra, my center of self-esteem. After a few minutes, the color switched to light green, providing healing to my heart chakra. Finally, the color changed to a dark red giving healing to my first chakra, my energy center, symbolizing health, wealth, and stability in the world.

I then found myself back at the foot of God. I saw a visual reminder of Tiffany, a participant from the IANDS conference meditation I led. At the time of the conference, Archangel Michael told me that she might be instrumental in connecting me with a benefactor for Enlightened World. But, when the meditation was over, she realized another participant had walked out with her conference bag including her wallet. She ran off to track it down before I could speak directly with her.

God, am I supposed to connect with Tiffany again?
Yes.
Since she has my business card, and I don't have her contact information, will you be whispering in her ear to reach back out to me?
No.
Hmmm.
Will you ask Spirit to whisper in her ear reminding her to reach out to me?
Yes.
Are you teaching me to say exactly what I want from you in prayer?

229

Yes.

I remembered our youngest daughter playing make-believe as a waitress when she was three years old. After perusing our refrigerator and cupboards, she created a "menu." She walked up, handed us the menu, and very clearly announced, "What you name, what you want?" The more precise our reply, the better the chances of getting what we requested. Okay then.

God, you have shown me several projects for Enlightened World that will need a benefactor, like our website development, the series of children's picture books on angels, and each of the conferences. Will you please let me know who I am to ask, have them reach out to me, or have a person who knows them connect with me somehow?

Yes.

Thank you. And so it is.

chapter twenty

Reach for the Light

Most of us do have a smaller vision of who we are, and in the world of spirit, they are very anxious for us to know how much bigger we are and to step into that.
-Sumaya O'Grady, Soul Alchemist

As Divine Mother reminded me, we are supposed to be expanding our light to become more God-like. Not that we are striving to be God, as that role is already taken. But if we are in tune with Spirit and each stand in the light of our Source, our God, our universal energy, then I believe we, in concert, can create a ripple effect on the planet. I appreciate all that each one of you is doing to bring more light to the world. You are needed right now more than ever. The following vignettes are provided as inspiration to you as you proceed along your journey.

STAND IN DIVINE WHITE LIGHT

As souls in bodies, we always have free will. Our ability to grow into knowing and loving Spirit, and to evolve into the soul we were intended to be, are always options for us. Every morning that we wake up, every conversation we have, presents us with the choice to either dig deep into the lower level energies or soar into what your soul is here on earth to become.

When I wake up in the morning, the very first thing that I do is check in with Spirit. And then I open my crown wide to God's pure white light only, because frankly, that's the only light I want anymore. For fun, I used to clear my energy by bringing down the different colors of light that were associated with the different chakras. I quickly tired of that. So now, I just sit in God's presence, and I will listen to see if there is a message or lesson that I am supposed to learn. Sometimes, it's just a downpour of divine energy into my being, and I can do that anywhere I am. I can do that if I am sitting on the freeway or standing in a grocery store checkout line, and all I need to do is ground myself through my feet or my chair, and open myself up to God's immense presence and healing light.

Pure divine healing light is all I want running through me. I want people to see the divine healing light running through me and want that for themselves. That which I have experienced is available to others; all they need to do is to seek it.

IT'S OKAY TO BE A LIGHTHOUSE

I had a reading scheduled with a beautiful soul, Gianna, and her son Marco, from Italy. As I drove home to prepare for our Skype session, I was thinking of Gianna and our upcoming time together. Just then, three white doves flew right in front of my windshield and made themselves seen. It felt like a message for Gianna, and I promised that I would tell her that when we spoke.

When I looked at Gianna's energy, I saw that she was very connected to God, Jesus, Divine Mother, and the archangels. Her attention was being distracted by a child pulling around her neck saying, "Look at me!"

I heard the word, *"Patience."* Looking at her son Marco's energy, I saw that his energy was frenetic as if lightning was pulsing through his body. I saw anger and angst that he could not control, making it difficult for him to calm himself.

When I connected with Giana on Skype, I told her the things I had seen energetically. I described the three doves and that I wasn't sure if they were a sign for her or for me, but to me, they represented the Trinity. She reassured me that they were definitely a sign for her, as she had been praying for a sign that I worked with God and was a safe person for her to work with.

Gianna is a budding lightworker who doesn't know her own strength, other than the fact that all of her electronics go out when she is near. Her concern was six-year-old Marco and his behavioral issues. I saw that Gianna was not able to spend the time she wanted on her energetic pursuits because all of her time was consumed with him. I was given a vision of a lighthouse. A lighthouse simply stands there and shines so boat captains can navigate to safety. Lighthouses don't go out looking for boats to save. As a lightworker, she could stand in her energy and God's divine white light. Others could see and feel her presence and be impacted by that.

At the time of Marco's birth, Gianna was given the vision of an alien from another planet entering our universe. I said that I saw her son, as many others, as a hybrid of human/alien and that he had not been on our planet before. His learning curve was enormous, as he had no residual wisdom of how things work here on earth, from previous lifetimes. As a newbie, he was bound to be overwhelmed, and frankly, he looked like an easy target for boys looking for someone to tease. I was shown that Gianna should see her son as a spiritual being first, and then as a physical being. He has a great deal to learn. She said that Marco is fearful when she talks about grounding techniques. I explained that she might have better success working with him spirit to spirit. As he is still a child, she can simply ground him herself, and that will buy her time for when he is ready and able to learn energetic techniques as a physical being. Because I saw that he was an empath, I suggested she ask for four warrior angels to help protect him energetically.

Gianna was going through a divorce. When I brought in the father's energy to see how their energies worked together, Marco got very small out of fear and got right next to Gianna and put his energy through her like a blade. He called out, "Why aren't you protecting me from him?" We discussed the dynamics between father and son and what she could do to protect Marco. She described the father as having low level energies. I saw that Marco stood as a lighthouse in juxtaposition to the father's denser energies. I saw that this could be making the father uncomfortable and angry. I saw that in the future, when Marco is in his late teens and as an adult, that their relationship will be stronger and that the father will be able to accept his son's higher level frequencies.

As an adult, I saw Marco working alongside Gianna as a lightworker, like her. But for now, her job is to raise her son and future partner and teach him as a spiritual being, keeping him physically safe and helping him get acclimated to our world. The message of "*Patience*" was for Gianna. Spirit encouraged her to have patience and know that all will work out in the end.

In Left Field

Sometimes, I feel like I am out in left field all by myself. But that's ok! I am following my calling. And it is so okay for you to follow your own calling as well. Not only ok, but imperative! The world needs each of us to be conscious about fulfilling our purpose, even though our callings don't look like anyone else's. And because our callings don't look like anyone else's, it is even more imperative that we all participate! By following your calling, doing what you came here to do, it shows others that it is okay for them to be all that they are meant to become. So please, be brave, stand in your light, and follow your calling. We are counting on you!

Pieces of the Whole

We are energetically all pieces of one whole. Imagine many blades of grass connected to the same root system. When we send love through thought or deed to others, we send love to ourselves as well.

The Here and Now

I am reminded of the importance of the here and now. Aside from the things that I have to do on any given day, I always make time to sit and check in with my guides and angels. If I am thinking about the past, I cannot check in with my guides because they exist only in real time. If I am thinking about the future, I can't connect with them either. The only way I can communicate with them is if I am in the present. As my thoughts travel to my children, husband, parents, and friends, I believe the same could be said. The only way to truly connect with another being, in the physical or in the spiritual realm, is to have my thoughts focusing on them in the here and now.

Note to self: Don't limit your present experiences by living in the past or future. Don't waste precious time focusing on the future, as we never know how the future will play itself out.

The Holidays

Some of us go into the holidays with our arms and hearts outstretched, cheering, "Bring it on!" Others of us face the holidays with dread, feelings of grief, or outright disdain. These are all very natural and honest sentiments.

For those of you walking into the holidays with heavy hearts, I truly understand. There is nothing like the holidays to shine a spotlight on things we wish were different.

On occasion, when I have preferred to wallow in hurt or isolation, it eventually started to feel like more effort to stay unhappy. I learned that I have the choice to work at staying unhappy or work at trying to find love and grace in the moment. Either way, it is energy expended on my part. Every moment, every conversation, I have the option of sinking into the depths or embracing the light. Some heart-wrenching days I find myself vacillating between wallowing in the hurt and embracing the light. I guess it's all part of being human. In my more rational moments I realize that when I choose the love and grace route, I feel much lighter and at peace. I hope that you will be gentle with yourselves as each holiday season comes around.

Incoming Reinforcement

When I seek to replenish my energy by myself without going upward to Spirit, I very quickly become depleted. It reminds me of riding in a car with the air on recirculate. It doesn't take long for the air to seem stale. But, when I connect with the divine healing light of God, it is much easier to replenish my stamina. The archangels and the Divine Mother are there, and we each can connect with them any time we want. All we have to do is ask.

Due North

My husband and I went looking at new cars the other day. One of them had a large compass on the dashboard. I don't know about you, but my driving habits don't require a compass. It was distracting that it was always in view, taking up a large piece of real estate on the dashboard. But then I got thinking. As a spiritual being, I use a compass daily. As I plan my day, build my business and my relationships, I align myself with my higher self, my soul's calling, and Spirit. As my path has become more solidly defined in front of me, I rely on my spiritual North Star even more.

Going Home

When I meditate, I close my eyes and imagine that I am in that place in my heart that I call home. Rarely, is it in my actual house. Sometimes my location changes, but often it is in the loft in the Nantucket rental home. I immerse myself in the feelings, memories, sights, and sounds of my "home." I suppose because I am intuitive, it is easy for me to put myself right back into that energy. It is a sneaky way to feel like I have been on vacation while I sit in my bedroom. I find that starting mediation from that place of comfort helps me relax, feel refreshed, and be open to the gifts the Universe has to offer. Find your place of joy and contentment, find your home, if only in your mind.

Dragonfly

The other morning, I drove to visit my mother at her assisted living facility. I was feeling emotionally fatigued, as watching her decline with dementia has been difficult. I know that the time I spend with her might provide the only full conversation or emotional connection she has all day. Spending time with her is not only important, but it is also a responsibility. As her conversations become an increasingly convoluted mix of reality, memories, and deluded thinking, it is harder for me to sit and listen.

I stepped out of my car and saw a large dragonfly on the ground next to a puddle of dirty water. Its wings were vibrating gently, and I could see it was unable to fly. I found a stiff piece of paper and gently scooped it up. I didn't touch it with my hands for fear I would cause further injury. I spoke to it as I moved it to a grassy area and laid it on a soft weed, hoping it would be able to fly at some point. I heard the words, "***Helping souls one at a time.***" Somehow it didn't seem so difficult to lift up just one soul. I saw Divine Mother next to me. As she symbolizes nature and the Divine Feminine, I knew the dragonfly was in good hands regardless of its outcome.

I thought to give the dragonfly Reiki. I envisioned it sitting in my hands as I contemplated the best way to provide the healing energy. I saw heavenly divine light coming down, surrounding and emanating through the dragonfly. Divine healing light being connected to the dragonfly's soul was the best healing it could possibly receive; whether it lived or died was not the important issue. Being one with the loving grace of God was the quintessential "I am." Other circumstances surrounding one's physicality were secondary.

My thoughts turned to my mother. Rather than getting bogged down in the realities of her dementia, could I merely lift her in spirit, envision her immersed in divine healing light, and in a spiritual connection to her divinity? Would that not be the most desirable thing for her right now? Helping souls one at a time. I can do this.

Spirit in Motion

One morning, I woke early and enjoyed the comfort of my bed in the darkness. I stayed in bed while I wrote the curriculum for my radio podcasts. In the dusky light, I heard a dove calling from the front of the house. That's funny; I haven't heard a dove here for over a year. It triggered fond memories and immediately brought peace and love to my heart.

I looked on the internet to see what the dove symbolized: "The dove represents peace of the deepest kind. It soothes and quiets our worried or troubled thoughts, enabling us to find renewal in the silence of the mind. The dove's singing is most prevalent when the veils between the physical and spiritual worlds are thought to be at their thinnest – first thing in the morning and the last thing at night – again representing a link between two divergent domains. Doves teach us that, regardless of external circumstances, peace is always a touch away – within us – and always available." http://www.pure-spirit.com

I sat and sank into the sounds of the dove. I felt Sylvia's presence join me, my dear friend, who passed several years ago, and I was emotionally transported into a memory that we shared. One summer, while I was working on my doctorate, I visited her in Hawaii for ten days. Every morning I woke at 4:00, sat in bed and wrote my doctoral dissertation. I got in six or more hours of uninterrupted writing until Sylvia was awake and ready to enjoy the day. Each morning when I woke it was dark out. By about 5:00 there was a hint of light triggering the birds to start singing. Their serenade echoed throughout the hills of the neighborhood, and it sounded like the birds were convening outside my window. There were songbirds with beautiful, melodious voices and a lot of doves. Their singing was quite loud for about 10 minutes, I would stop writing, not because I meant to, but because my heart, brain, and spirit would get carried away with the wonder, the beauty, and gift of the moment. Tears came to my eyes with gratitude. Here I was in the paradise of Hawaii with the person I was closest to in the world, with no responsibilities except writing and having fun, and surrounded by this amazing gift from nature. Every morning I looked forward to this time.

Here 21 years later, I was transported into these memories as if they were yesterday. I remember that time with Sylvia with such fondness and gratitude. The term "Spirit in Motion" came to my mind describing that time of my life when I was in clear alignment with my purpose, my heart, and my spirit. Everything was in sync and as it should be.

I felt Sylvia's presence join me reminding me of the specialness of that time together. She showed me that she is with me now while I am walking through my life's journey. And once again I am Spirit in Motion.

Taking Flight

My neighbor, Norma, and I met over breakfast to discuss the possibility of writing a children's book on angels together. Our time was rich with Spirit sharing idea after idea. We were so inspired that one book had morphed into a series of twelve, each one focusing on an archangel. In one short hour, we had all twelve books mapped out. The synergy of our ideas was highlighted by the loving acknowledgment time and again by Spirit that we were not only on the right track but that the ideas were divinely inspired.

As we stepped out of the restaurant, we saw an eagle flying low, circling over our heads. An eagle that close to downtown was an unusual sight. I quickly pulled out my phone and looked up the symbolism of the eagle spirit. It read, "When an eagle appears, you are on notice to be courageous and stretch your limits. Do not accept the status quo, but rather reach higher and become more than you believe you are capable of. Look at things from a new perspective. Be patient with the present; know that the future holds possibilities that you may not yet be able to see. You are about to take flight." www.pure-spirit.com

Parting Gifts

I sat on my patio enjoying the early morning light. Wind jostled the aspen leaves and created dancing shadows on the ground. My eye traveled to two Japanese lanterns under the aspen tree. The lanterns in the dancing light looked enchanting against the backdrop of the aspen tree. I watched the light and movement transfixed for several minutes. I wanted to remember the magic of the moment, so I snapped a few photos.

When I looked back at the photos, there was a faint streak of a rainbow prism across the front of the lanterns. I asked Divine Mother about what I saw.

Divine Mother, was that a sign from you?

Yes.

Divine Mother, are rainbows a sign from you?

Yes.

I remembered what I learned about rainbows. I was told that the rainbow pointing to land at Noah's Ark was not a sign from God.

Divine Mother, was the rainbow at Noah's Ark a sign from God?

No.

Was the rainbow at Noah's Ark a sign from you?

Yes.

Aww. That is beautiful! Divine Mother, thank you for listening.
You are welcome.
I saw a vision of Christ.
As Christ is my son, you are my daughter.
I know it is different, but thank you.
I love you.
I love you.

About the Author

Dr. Ruth Anderson is an award-winning author, Ordained Minister and founder of Enlightened World. Retired after a satisfying and worthwhile career in public school administration, Ruth embraced her second calling, that of intuitive, spiritual counselor, speaker, and author. She has devoted her retirement to striving to live a high vibrational existence and making a difference in the spiritual lives of others. Her passion and purpose are to serve as a conduit between the spiritual realm and the physical realm, sharing knowledge gained from direct experience, and educating others along the way. Ruth is passionate about sharing energetic concepts and her experiences with the Spiritual Divinity. She sees her writing and speaking as an extension of the contract she has with Spirit to learn and share with others. She writes a recurring column for the Shelton Mason County Journal.

An avid writer, Ruth contributes to publications and anthologies while authoring her books. Her first narrative, One Love: Divine Healing at Open Clinic won awards in the areas of Inspirational,

Religion & Spirituality, Angels & Spirit Guides, Psychic Phenomena, Supernatural, and Spiritual Healing. She later authored Walking with Spirit: Divine Illuminations on Life, Death and Beyond. A spiritual counselor, Dr. Anderson provides individualized, transformational experiences creating connections with the Spiritual Divinity including Divine Mother, Archangels Michael, Gabriel and Raphael, and incorporating Holy Fire Reiki, and energy work.

Contributing Author:
- *Chicken Soup for the Soul: Miracles and More*
- *Chicken Soup for the Soul: Messages from Heaven and Other Miracles*
- International Best Seller *Warrior Women with Angel Wings for the Soul*
- International Best Seller *Warrior Women with Angel Wings Born to Love*
- Best Seller *Warrior Women with Angel Wings for the Soul Illuminate Your Joy*
- International Best Seller *Step Forward and Shine*
- International Best Seller *Empowering You, Transforming Lives*

Follow Dr. Anderson at www.theministryonline.org
Facebook: www.facebook.com/theministryonline1
She may be contacted at openclinic1@gmail.com.

Reviews

As a woman in midlife who has now lived half of her childhood, and most of her life without her mother, I read "Listening to Light" with a growing sense of hope, encouragement, and eventually delight. The theme of Divine Mother is at the heart of this rich, helpful, and inspiring book. Not far in, I began to feel like it was written just for me. The death of my mother at the hands of a hit-and-run-driver all those decades ago led to emotional devastation for me, but also a profound spiritual crisis. It was above all a dark night of the soul.

Yet it also led to an eventual reawakening. I decided that perhaps I could re-establish a relationship with the Goodness in life. I found therapy, fulfilling work, got a doctorate, became a mother. Soon after, I became a Quaker and found warmth in a community of Friends. I eventually trained as a grief coach, and read far and wide about grief, positive psychology, neuroscience, and evidence-based coaching. There was now meaning, purpose, and love in my life again.

But something was still off. I'd never truly been able to shake off a lingering feeling that I could lose everything in an instant, especially if things were going well, like a shadow that looms larger when the sun is out. Despite everything I'd read or heard about from spiritually awakened people, I still suspected that, unlike them, I was doomed to a secretive, uneasy, co-dependent relationship with a judgmental, angry Man in the Sky.

Years of personal development had, of course, led to an awareness of my shadow thinking and even the adoption of new, more empowered ways of thinking, on a thought-by-thought basis. But what I needed was a new relationship with Goodness, a new vision of Goodness.

As I was reading *Listening to Light,* it felt like a remembering of what I had once known to be true. I'd even read many books about re-embracing the spiritual feminine. This time, however, the writing was about one woman's personal and developing relationship with the Divine Mother, moment by moment, as part of the Spiritual Divinity.

I began to form some new questions:

- What if I too could find unconditional warmth, love, and encouragement from Divine Mother?
- What if I could build a relationship with Divine Mother in all her forms of expression?
- What if Divine Mother is there wherever I find compassion, nurturing, and kindness, not only in others but also in myself?
- What if Divine Mother could be whispering to me as the sound of leaves rustling in the trees? Or connecting to me when I see a statue of Mary? Walking gently on Mother Earth? Listening to another with patience and kindness? Or keeping my heart open, even when painful, as the mother of a teenager?

All these could be times of worship, times of prayer, of connection--sacred moments in an unfolding relationship with the unconditional love that is Divine Mother. Divine Mother is calling to be restored to her rightful place in my heart, and, I pray, in the heart of us all.

-Dido Clark, PhD

Ruth Anderson's newest book is a love letter to the Light that the Divine Source and the Divine Feminine shine down onto and through all of creation. It is also a beautiful gift to those reading, offering personal stories of the learning and listening required to enable each of us to personally walk with and in Spirit. A lovely read and important message regardless of where one is on his or her journey.

-Nancy Tarr Hart, PhD

Dr. Ruth Anderson is a visionary, open channel for the Light and deeply compassionate spiritual teacher for love in this time of a great shifting in awareness on our planet. Her new book, *Listening to Light: Love Letters from Walking with Spirit* is an incredibly beautiful testament to the power and grace in the human spirit and our ability to connect to Divine Mother and the Archangels for guidance and help in our mission here on earth.

Ruth has a way of connecting Spirit to all aspects of our lives and her love letters are a gift of awakening into the light for all who read them.

Ruth has the most wonderful clarity and way of assisting us in very practical ways, from showing us how to receive guidance, to knowing how to apply it in profound and meaningful ways.

She connects us to Spiritual Divinity and helps us to find our place in this world as a lightworker. What a gift this book is! "Just love", she says and know, as Christ was the son, so we are the sons and daughters of Divine Mother.

Her stories touch the deepest part of what is human and divine in us. From the opening 'Love Letters' to being "a Light" for this world, Ruth weaves her love and light throughout by providing a strong foundation and understanding of Spiritual Divinity, and helping us to see and get to know the energy and the light and what is in store for us in this precious human life. She shares what it means to listen and heal and how to deal with obstacles and tough days as well as loving and sharing the language of the heart. Fundamentally she helps us to connect to our calling and connect to Spirit in a way that helps us to stand clearly in the Divine Light.

I unequivocally recommend *Listening to Light: Love Letters from Walking with Spirit* to all people as a gift from God, Divine Mother, and the Archangels. A gift that will change your life and lift you up to fly in pure Spirit.

-Stephen Skelton Altair

It has become more essential than ever to connect to Divine Mother and bring compassion, nourishment and palpable love to ourselves and others. In Listening to Light: Love Letters from Walking with Spirit, Ruth shares her dialogue with God, Divine Mother and Archangels as she receives more understanding and validation on her journey as a lightworker. She teaches us how to connect to Divine Light and how through group meditation we can make our spirit energy stronger so healing can be more far-reaching. Her message shows us that the light can begin in each of us. We can open our hearts and seek our own spiritual purpose and enlightenment. Thanks, Ruth, for helping guide us to begin this greatest journey.

-Kathleen Marie

Dr Ruth Anderson's book Listening to Light: Love Letters from Walking with Spirit is a wonderful combination of spiritual teachings as well as following Ruth's spiritual journey in her connections, learnings and receiving message from the Divine, including God, the Divine Mother, Jesus, Holy Spirt and the Archangels Michael, Gabriel, Uriel and Cassiel, in order for her to write this book that you now have before you (or hold in your hands). Her book is very inspiring as well as encouraging for us to connect with the Divine in our own everyday lives to help to make our life's path and everyday a blessing, as we follow the guidance that we receive with trust, love and grace.

-Rachel Cooley

Her best book yet, this is so insightful to God's love for us, directly from the source... how pure is that! Dr. Ruth Anderson is truly a friend of God, sharing God's light and love with all of us. Her life's purpose is to help us to be the very best humans that we can be by helping us to raise our consciousness and heal our hearts. Listening to Light: Love Letters from Walking with Spirit reminds us that God's love and light are accessible and available to ALL of us. We just need to invite God into our hearts. -Denice MarieOnce again, Dr. Ruth Anderson sweeps you into her story as archangels, Divine Mother and Holy Spirit share the meaning of divine light, energy, the significance of our soul's colors and Christ Consciousness. With her characteristic warmth and grace Ruth takes you beyond the veil as these divine beings communicate through her to spread the message of hope, purpose and higher consciousness for everyone. This is a jewel among Ruth's three books. It left me captivated, uplifted and hungry for more. Read it now to achieve greater personal discovery and understanding of your world.

-Linda Dierks